humor
me

**AMERICA'S FUNNIEST
HUMORISTS ON THE
POWER OF LAUGHTER**

Copyright © 2003 BMP Publications

Printed in the USA

Cover and Page Design by Connection Graphics

Published by:

Brad Montgomery, CSP
Brad Montgomery Productions
Denver, CO
800.624.4280

ISBN: 0-9743490-0-1

This book is sold with the understanding that the subject matter is of a general nature and does not constitute medical, legal, or other professional advice for any specific individual or situation. Readers planning to take action in any areas that this book describes should seek professional advice from their doctors, specialists, and other advisors, as would be prudent or advisable under their given circumstances.

Additional copies of *Humor Me* can be obtained by any of the authors in this book. Contact information follows each chapter.

Acknowledgments

This book is a great example of how many people working together can produce something better than someone working alone.

I am grateful to the other 15 authors in this book who are more than just funny people. They are mentors, speakers, performers and friends. I am more flattered by and appreciative of their participation in *Humor Me* than they will ever guess.

Eric Chester, CSP, is a wonderful speaker, author and publisher. He is also a mentor who generously shared his extensive and valuable experience and insight. I am enormously grateful for his help, advice, and generosity.

Vilis Ozols, MBA, CSP, is always available for advice, support, and concrete suggestions. His big-heartedness is overwhelming and very much appreciated.

Thanks to Connie Sweet and John Strpko of Connection Graphics for making this book look beautiful. To Barbara McNichol, who is more than our editor; she is a valuable advisor, helper, and friend. To Bob Eubanks who agreed to review this book and share his endorsement. Also to Kim Wooldridge, Paulette Wasserstein, and Caitlin Lillie for their constructive and important help along the way.

And finally, thanks to my family, Kim, Claire, Ben, and Paige. They keep me laughing.

- Brad Montgomery,
  Publisher and Contributing Author

Table of Contents

Introduction

The book you hold in your hand is not a joke book—although it will make you laugh. It's not a book about comedy technique—but it can help you be funnier. It is a book about the power of laughter and humor, about the importance and value of having fun. And it's a book chock-full of tips on how to inject more humor into your life—starting today!

Why This Book?

The everyday stresses of life can leave us feeling hassled, hurried, and tightly wound. Add to that a fragile economy during a time of threatened security, and we could be left feeling frightened, vulnerable, and off the chart on the stress meter. We need tools for coping.

Humor and laughter are two of the best. Not only do they make life more enjoyable, they help us deal more effectively with real-life difficulties we may face.

Within these pages, you'll find tons of information on using humor to manage the stress of change, loss, conflict, disability, and even death. You'll learn how to use humor to deal effectively with others, to strengthen relationships, and to encourage people to join you in the process. Humor and laughter will not just change your day; they can change your life.

Why These Authors?

When you want to learn about something, you check with an expert, right? Lucky you! With *Humor Me*, you hold in your hands the wisdom of not one, but 16 experts on the power of laughter and humor.

These authors do much more than make their closest pals laugh. They can take any group, on any day, anywhere, and shake them out of their chairs with laughter. Their craft requires study, practice, and a deep understanding of human nature as they apply humor toward putting us in step with our lives.

Not only are these authors VERY funny, but they also have hundreds of years of combined experience in teaching others why laughter reduces the ill effects of stress. Their stories and examples show you how to reap the rewards that come from living your life with more humor.

Humor Me is written by some of the most experienced professionals in America. You'll see alphabet soup following their names because higher education and advanced degrees are plentiful among this group. But you might not recognize two designations, both awarded by the National Speakers Association. In the world of experts who speak professionally, these two recognized symbols of excellence are the Certified Speaking Professional (CSP) and the Council of Peers Award for Excellence (CPAE).

The CSP designation is conferred only on those who have met strict criteria regarding experience, professionalism, and platform skills. Fewer than 7% of professional speakers worldwide have earned this designation. And *Humor Me* features 11 CSPs.

The CPAE Speaker Hall of Fame signifies the top echelon of platform excellence and professionalism. The CPAE is a big deal. Actually, it's huge. And two authors in *Humor Me* have CPAE behind their names. (For more information on these designations and the National Speakers Association, visit www.nsaspeaker.org.)

Why Now?

Why put up with unnecessary stress for one more minute when there's something you can do about it that's fun, free, and fairly easy to learn? There's no time like *now* to think, laugh, and learn. Go ahead. Turn the page and get started!

MIRTHMAKING
It's A Distance Thing

by Mark Mayfield, CSP, CPAE

I get asked all the time, "Do you try to make a joke out of everything?" Of course not; there was that one time back in '87 when I accidentally took too many painkillers for a pinched nerve and I was in a brain fog and I didn't try to make a joke out of my cat eating the neighbor's parakeet. But that's about it. Other than that one moment, I pretty much try to make a joke out of everything. It's my job.

I make mirth. I won't get hung up on semantics, but mirth is humor. Humor is mirth. I'm not going to spend any time dissecting the nuances of each word because as the old saying goes, dissecting humor is like dissecting a frog — nobody really enjoys it and the frog dies. So if you want to get into some esoteric, interplanetary, higher meaning of these words . . . *stop reading now*. Ain't gonna happen. I'm just using the word mirth because it's different and it's cool.

The Gladness and Laughter Duo

Mirth is gladness accompanied by laughter. You gotta have both of those ingredients for mirth — gladness *and* laughter. If you just have one, you've missed the point. Imagine Abbot without Costello, peaches without cream, reality shows without idiots. None of these duos works well without both components. The same is true with mirth. You must have both gladness *and* laughter. If you have gladness with no laughter, you get none of the physiological benefits of laughter. And there are hordes of documented evidence of these benefits. On the other hand, if you laugh without the gladness, you may feel good physically, but you'll have no perspective of the situation and your problems will defeat you. Let me explain.

At Arm's Length

Mirthmaking has many benefits, but at the top of my list is the fact that mirth gives you distance. If you place the palm of your open hand against your nose, you see nothing but a big ol' blob of blur. Nothing is in focus. But what do you see if you stretch your arm out at full length? If you still see a big ol' blob of blur, you need an optometrist; but most of you will see your hand in focus. All you did was create distance. This is a great metaphor for the power of mirth.

Mirth gives you distance—from problems and daily stressors. And in case you didn't know, life is much easier to handle (and lots more fun) when you can see things from a distance. A problem can be overwhelming when the *problem* is all you see. Your heart rate rises, blood pressure soars, and respiration gets poor. In technical terms, it's a bad thing.

When you have distance, you have perspective. Perspective means seeing all the angles and options, and not just what's up front. It means seeing the whole picture. Is the glass half empty or half full? From a mirth perspective, it's neither. The glass is too dang big! Hey, knucklehead, get a smaller glass and it'll be full. That's the mirth perspective — you see more angles. You can only do that with distance.

So how does mirth give you distance? The answer is simple. It opens your mind. That's why it enhances your creativity. Your sense of humor and your sense of creativity are virtually the same thing. Both of those senses involve seeing many options, rather than just the obvious. Mirth and creativity are like two lobes of the brain sitting next to each other. Mirth is the "Ha-Ha"; creativity is the "Ah-Ha."

White Shoes with Sass

A few years ago, I was in my hotel room getting ready for an engagement when I realized I had forgotten to pack dress shoes. It was summer and I had driven my car to this meeting. When I drive in the summer, I drive comfortably. I wear big baggy shorts, a big baggy t-shirt, and white loafers. But as I'm getting ready to go on stage, I realized these white loafers are the only shoes I have with me. I have a dark double-breasted suit and white shoes. I look sassy! No I don't. I look like an idiot.

I panicked, went downstairs, and tried to cajole the bellman out of his shoes. (I used the word "cajole" here to give you a word to look up in the dictionary. You can get extra credit for this. Go ahead, do this now so you know the correct definition and pronunciation. Okay, let's continue.) I had no luck cajoling him out of his shoes. He did, however, inform me of a clothing store across the street that carried shoes. I didn't have time to race upstairs and change, so I scurried into this clothing store wearing a dark suit and white shoes. It was like Pat Boone making a comeback. As I entered through the door, I looked at the storeowner and asked, "What do you suppose I need?" His answer was swift: "A white suit?"

My first impression was that this guy was very funny, but when you think about it, he's much more than that. While I certainly admire his ability to make mirth, it's his creativity that will put more money in his pocket. He knows the margin or profit on selling me a suit is far greater than on a pair of shoes. Mirth and creativity are nearly synonymous; using one builds the other. So if you want to enhance your creativity, make a little mirth.

Silly Signs

That's the value of distance. You see more. That's what mirth can do for you—you'll see more possibilities, you'll see the whole picture, and you'll see a better way to do things. So if you want to experience all those things, start by seeing the funny stuff.

Here's an example of what I'm talking about. My post office has a sign that says, *No Dogs Allowed, Except For Seeing Eye Dogs.* Do they really need to state that exception? I don't think a blind person is going to *read* the sign and say, "Okay, Rover, it's okay for you to come on in." Probably dozens of times you've seen the sign *For Sale by Owner.* Look at it with mirth. Of course it's for sale by the owner. That's a basic tenet in this country. You must own it before you sell it. What are the other options? *For Sale by Renter* or *For Sale by Mad Neighbor.* Look past the obvious. Make mirth. It will give you distance because it'll open your mind.

Shortening the Distance

There is one huge exception to this distance thing. Mirth gives you distance from problems, emotions, places, and things, but not from people. It actually brings you closer to people. It shortens the distance between people. Mirth knows no barriers like age, race, gender, or education. People like people who can make mirth; probably because it has a great way of reducing tension among people.

A few years ago, I witnessed a medical emergency on an airplane. The woman across the aisle from me experienced a heart attack. My medical expertise is limited to diagnosing a hangnail, but even I knew what was going on here. Fortunately a physician on board was able to stabilize her and move her to the front of the aircraft. I've never seen people sit on a plane so quietly.

We landed in Chicago and taxied to the terminal. As we hooked up to the jet way, the flight attendant asked all the passengers to remain in their seats until the paramedics had removed the medical emergency. I hate to be redundant, but I can't describe how silent it was on the plane. Everyone knew it was a life-and-death situation.

The hushed atmosphere was then disrupted by a man behind me who stood up and said, "Fine, just fine. Hey, I know she's got problems; we've all got problems. I've got to get off of this plane right now and make a connection to Los Angeles and I do mean right now. I don't care what kind of problem anybody has." This guy was a real jerk and a complete waste of skin. He was yelling at the flight attendant and the tension was major thick.

That's when a man a few rows ahead of me and far more witty than I stood up, looked at the jerk behind me, and said, "Hey buddy, if I ever have a heart transplant, I want yours, because it's never been used." The entire plane erupted in applause and laughter. The tension evaporated. Everybody on that plane connected, even the jerk. He realized how inconsiderate he'd been and declared, "Sorry, I'm guilty," and then sat down.

Mirth can remove tension as well as anything. Did you ever try to be mad at someone while you're laughing with him or her? It's impossible. My favorite quote about laughter is the one credited to Victor Borge, "Laughter is the shortest distance between two people."

Dirty Shirts

Not long ago, I was heading to the airport and I stopped at the drycleaners on the way. I was going to be gone two weeks so I needed both of my shirts. (Maybe I shouldn't have put that bit of personal hygiene information in this chapter.) When I was handed my shirts, I could see that both were in unacceptable condition. One of them still had a stain and the other looked like someone had ironed it with an asphalt roller. I wasn't happy. I yelled at the owner. I told him this was absurd, ridiculous, and awful, and lots of other words I can't put here. I told him that I was heading out of town with bad shirts and wanted to know what he was going to do about it.

He looked at me, gathered himself, and calmly said, "You're absolutely right. We're 100% at fault here. I know the lady who cleaned these shirts and there is only one thing we can do. We'll shoot her. It's my mom and I'm gonna miss her, but we gotta do it."

Was there any way I could stay mad at this guy? No way. I was on the floor howling. Simply said, mirth reduces tension.

Get Off the Floor

So how can you make mirth to create space from problems, yet narrow the space between people? Simple. Steve Allen used to say that the world is a comedy room. Some people are on the floor and some are on the ceiling. The people on the ceiling are the Robin Williamses and Whoopi Goldbergs of the world; the people on the floor are easy to spot as well. They always find what's wrong with the situation. If it's a beautiful day outside they say, "Well, it means there's a nasty one around the corner."

You don't have to be on the ceiling to make mirth. Just get off the floor. And I'm not suggesting you start telling jokes or wear Groucho Marx glasses or put plastic throw-up on seats. (Okay, that last one I am suggesting, it works every single time.) It just means to get up off the floor and make a little mirth. You can do this if you'll occasionally lighten up and be a kid. Kids have open minds with voracious creativity.

Be a Kid at Heart

One of my best friends has a four-year-old son who recently asked him, "Was Humpty Dumpty's mom a big fat chicken?" Only a kid would think of that. So be a kid at heart. If at no other time of the year, you have the opportunity on Halloween. It's a chance to dress up and act like a kid.

Last year I was a ballerina. I even had the tights and a tutu. Apparently, many folks haven't seen a 185-pound ballerina with a potbelly because small children were frightened, and I don't mean in a spooky way, but in a "he's very strange" way. By next Halloween, however, the restraining orders will have expired and I'll have another chance to celebrate this great holiday.

You don't stop playing because you grow old; you grow old because you stop playing.

Look at Yourself

If being a kid is too difficult for you, I have a simpler solution. In the morning when you wake up, wipe the sleep from your eyes, march into the bathroom, and stare at yourself...naked. After you cry for a while, keep staring. I guarantee you this sight will make you laugh.

There are many beautiful creatures on this planet, like a white Bengal tiger or a racing thoroughbred, but you and I naked do not fit into the "beautiful" category. If you don't believe that we're funny-looking creatures, try to explain the spare hair that's placed on the back of men (and my Aunt Myrtle). Now I don't even know you, but I do know *me* and I can assure you, I ain't beautiful when I'm naked.

What am I saying? I'm saying you need to laugh at yourself. You are a wealth of comedic material and you do laughable stuff all the time. It just means you're normal. Have you ever called someone and, when they answered the phone, you'd forgotten who you called? Sure you have. In that instance, you have to ask, "Who is this?" They may say something like, "It's your mother."

Or how about when you're looking for something? While you're in the process of looking for it, you completely forget what you are looking for. What do you do then? You just keep on looking, don't you? Do you think you're just going to bump into it or something?

Or how about when you get in your car after it's been sitting out all day in cold weather? You know the engine is cold and you know the heater takes a while to warm up, but you still immediately turn the heater fan on "high." Now you've got a wind chill factor in the car.

We all do goofy stuff all the time. They provide great ways to make mirth — to laugh at yourself. I've been watching people a long time and there's one thing I know for sure: We're all idiots. That's how you know if you are normal. If you do silly stuff — you're normal. So laugh at yourself

In Review

Get off the floor.

Be a kid.

Look at yourself naked.

Pretty simple, huh?

About the Author

Mark Mayfield, CSP, CPAE

A former corporate lobbyist and nightclub performer, Mark is one of America's finest humorists. Content-based and comedy-driven, his presentations address serious stuff in a hilarious way. He is the author of the popular book *Mom's Rules,* a comedic yet poignant look at those things "Mom" said to us when we were kids. Mark has been called "one of the very few, really funny, thought-provoking people in America today." (His mother also said that after a small bribe.)

Mark has earned the Certified Speaking Professional designation and CPAE Speaker Hall of Fame recognition from the National Speakers Association.

Contact Information:

Mark Mayfield, CSP, CPAE
Mayfield Presentations
407 Lakeview Drive
Smithville, MO 64089

Phone: 816-532-8702
www.markmayfield.com
E-mail: Mark@markmayfield.com

How Humor *Made* My Life

by Michael D. Aronin

Humor might not have *saved* my life, but it definitely *made* my life. At various turns, it has made my life bearable; at others, remarkable; at still others, joyful, committed, and amazing—at least to me.

This chapter touches on two key points. First, how humor became a survival mechanism allowing me to soar beyond most people's expectations. Second, how it led to my path in stand-up comedy and professional speaking.

I hope my stories will make you smile, think, reflect, and feel good. All these stories are true—and I have copies of the police reports to prove it.

I was born and raised on Long Island, New York, in West Hempstead. I moved to Maryland for my college years at Towson University. I entered college as an accounting major who couldn't even balance a checkbook, and eventually switched to psychology and went on to complete my master's degree in counseling.

Today, I'm a motivational speaker who performs comedy on the weekends. I'm also a father to three lovely children— Brandon, Sydney, and Jonathon. And I am very happily married to my second wife, the smart-mouthed Patricia. While this might not sound particularly remarkable to you, it does to me; I have managed to accomplish all this despite being born with cerebral palsy.

Life with Cerebral Palsy

Legend has it that when I was born, not only had the world stopped, but so had my breathing. By the time the doctor resuscitated me, some of my brain cells hadn't received a full measure of oxygen. This lack of oxygen can cause the nerve damage associated with CP. Symptoms of CP vary widely, but I reflect those affecting speech and body movement.

Humor became a way for me to overcome the obstacles of CP. Not unlike a basketball career lifting a talented kid out of poverty, comedy became a vocation that allowed me to transcend what most people expected of me. It also was a tool for tweaking what could have been day-after-day heartbreak into a remarkably happy and funny life. I had to decide what to do with this lot that had been handed to me. Frankly, I chose to laugh about it.

I wasn't able to walk until I was four. One day, when I was about seven, I was walking through a department store with my mother and fell down. This wasn't surprising or unnerving to either of us since it was an every-other-day occurrence. But it was a shock to a woman standing near us. She rushed over to help and I waited until she was within earshot to say, "You know, Mom, I shouldn't have had that second drink this morning." It wasn't as funny later that day when Social Services pounded on our door.

Using Humor to Put People at Ease

Eventually I discovered humor not only helped me feel more comfortable in my own skin, but it helped others relax around me too. For many, that was often the first step toward their acceptance of someone they might have avoided.

When I walk on stage, I comment on my disability right away. How I do it depends on my mood. Sometimes I just smile at the audience for a few seconds. It gives us all a chance to get our bearings. Then I say something like, "I know what you're thinking. You see the way I walk, and you hear the way I talk, and I know you're wondering what it's like to be . . . Jewish."

After I deal with the CP and hear that first laugh break the ice, I tell the audience about growing up with cerebral palsy; that it actually had some advantages. (For one, I never had to clear the table at home.) I don't always touch on the CP issue. But, if I skip it, people think I am a character act. In those cases they come up to me after a performance, compliment me on a good show, and tell me I can "cut it out now."

Comedic Beginnings

How and why did I become a comic? My parents would like to know, too. (I can hear my mother crack, "Five years of tuition for this?") Well, it all started when I got divorced after a marriage that lasted just three and a half months. For some reason, my parents have always wanted to know more about that, too. And not only was my marriage ending, but my soon-to-be-ex-wife was pregnant. When we separated, I moved in with a fraternity brother who needed a roommate.

So there I was, living with a guy and feeling like crap about my life. I was in therapy, trying to rebuild my self-esteem and regain the positive attitude I'd had throughout my life. Then a woman I met bragged about this self-improvement course she'd just gone through. I took the course, and it was one of the best things I ever did. I felt unbelievably close to the people in the class and they convinced me I should do stand-up comedy. Looking back, I don't know whether to thank them or punch them in the nose. Maybe I should thank them *then* punch them in the nose.

I found an open mic night at a comedy club in Baltimore. The manager said he'd give me five minutes on the platform the following week. Dear God, how was I going to fill five minutes? How many "joke-jokes" did I know? But I *did* know what my opening line was going to be-"I got beaten up on the way in here. I took one of your parking spaces."

Suddenly the big open mic night arrived. I got to the club an hour before show time. The comics hung out in the back corner smoking and drinking. There were eight of them that night. Some were professional, some were regular open mic-ers, and some, like me, were giving it their first try.

I was sixth to go on. The room had a capacity of 150 but was just half-full that night. The audience seemed to be made up of friends of the comics. I didn't invite anyone because I knew that by stocking the audience with my friends, I'd never know how well I really did. With friends like mine, they might have told me I stunk when I was really the best thing since Jackie Mason.

The MC asked audience members to rate the show from one to ten, with ten being best. Before I went on, they were rating the show a six. After I went on, the score went up to a nine. Not bad for my first time on stage.

Well, that's not quite true. I *had* done talent shows as a kid. In the eighth grade, I came in second to a troupe of dancers. They went on to win Star Search, but I wasn't upset because Ed McMahon had just sent me a letter that said I might already be a winner. In high school, I did some comedy shows in nursing homes. In college, I won $100 in one talent contest when I wrote a top ten list of things overheard in the dining room. My number-one answer was "Let's call Domino's." That night during college, I first felt the excitement of a "real" performance.

Four years later, driving home from that club's open mic night with the most incredible natural high, that excitement of a "real" performance came back.

My First Paid Gig

I started going back to that club every week. I watched new comics and older, seasoned comics. Many times, I found myself wondering about the comics I'd admired who never returned. After my first open mic night, I received a call from the manager telling me a woman from Johns Hopkins University wanted to book me as the opening act at their health fair happy hour for 15 minutes. But I only had five minutes prepared—and that was if I did every single joke I had! Of course, I said yes. So there I was at Johns Hopkins, waiting to go on with two questions running through my mind: How do I follow a band? And how do I top the woman in the corner handing out free condoms?

I went up and told my jokes for about two minutes. The next 13 minutes felt like an eternity, but I got through them. Throngs of people screamed and cheered, or maybe that was just my mom who came down from New York by Amtrak. But what really inspired me was that even the professional comic who followed me on stage had only 20 minutes worth of material.

That night, I got paid a whopping $25. The check, still uncashed, hangs in a frame on my office wall. (I'm sorry if I screwed up the hospital's checkbook.) But hell, that night it was like I'd been struck by lightening. If I'd had hair, it would have been standing straight up.

Now, with one professional show under my belt, what was next?

I continued to go back to open mic night every week. Some nights, the crowds were large. Other nights, more comics filled the room than audience members. I hear that happens to Jay Leno, too. Hang in there, Jay! Keep your chin up!

But by that time, comedy had become my addictive drug. It got me through some very tough times - like becoming an ex-husband and a father almost within the same breath. And after many open mic nights at one particular club, the booker let me appear on a Thursday night with a line-up of professional comics. I did so well, the manager booked me for my first professional weekend. After that, I moved further into comedy, out of the open mic stage, and into more paying "gigs."

I don't mean to imply that I always do well on stage. I have, as they say, "eaten it" on many occasions. And it's actually good for me to eat it once in a while. It's a reminder that comedy is hard work. There will always be a new joke to write, timing to work out, and new ways to approach material. Whenever I write a new joke, I can't wait to try it out on stage. To me, it's like playing with a new toy. "Okay comedy world, here I am. When do you want me to do the Tonight Show?" Unfortunately, it's not as easy as making a phone call to Jay Leno and offering to take his place.

Being on stage is just a fraction of what it takes to become a comic. A comic has to do it over and over and over, then hope someone with the right connections happens to be watching. All I could think about was getting myself on stage in front of as many people as possible, even if their blood alcohol levels were higher than my grandmother's age.

Getting Started as a Motivational Speaker

After doing comedy for a year and half, another comic suggested I look into motivational speaking. I definitely had something to say that could help people, so I kicked the idea around for another year and half, then things just clicked. Now I speak for groups all over the country.

I love speaking professionally. I learn from the groups as much as the groups learn from me. But honing my ideas into something special enough to offer to large groups proved to be a long and difficult road, filled with trial and error.

Today, after six years in the speaking business, I continue to love what I do. As I speak, learn, and grow as an individual, my business flourishes as well. I'm serving another term on the Board of Directors of the National Speakers Association Washington D.C. chapter. I have been a member for six years and, as much as I give, my business grows in response. I feel such satisfaction when I welcome new members at a meeting and offer them the benefit of my experiences.

I'm seeing results from contacts I made two and three years ago. I now think that when businesses fail, it's not because the business-owners could not have succeeded, but because they got bogged down in the tough times of the present; they didn't force their heads up and envision the future. Six years in, I doubt I have broken even financially, but the outlook is definitely improving. What I envisioned so long ago is coming true.

Customer satisfaction keeps me going-that great feeling when audience members and I all sense that I've just "hit one out of the park." But please, don't think that I am cocky. I'm my own hardest critic. The flip side of that excitement of delivering a "real" performance can be hollow when someone tells me "great job" and I know deep inside it wasn't.

Over the last two years my stories have gotten stronger and my timing has improved. Not long ago, when I received a standing ovation, I thought the applause was because they appreciated that I didn't let adversity from CP get in my way.

Today when I receive a standing ovation, I know they're applauding the speech as well as the person who delivered it.

About the Author

Michael D. Aronin

Michael is a nationally acclaimed speaker who encourages people to improve their skills in the workplace while lifting their spirits and making them smile. Also a skilled comedian, he shows audience members how to get past personal shortcomings and move forward in their careers in entertaining and enlightening ways.

As a physically challenged member of the business community, Michael combines his personal experience with facts to provide a unique perspective on overcoming obstacles that goes far beyond "textbook knowledge."

Contact Information:

Michael Aronin
Rising Above
152 Langdon Farm Cr.
Odenton, MD 21113

Phone: 410.672.2565
www.michaelaronin.com

Developing Your Comic Vision™

by Tim Gard, CSP

Each year I meet people who tell me their goal is to "find the perfect job." I think they're surprised when I say no inherently perfect job awaits them because every job generates stress. But you can make yours more enjoyable by developing a Comic Vision.™

A Comic Vision™ is choosing to see the humor in situations instead of getting frustrated and angry when little things go wrong. It's not about telling jokes or using humor inappropriately; it is about harnessing laughter as a skill.

A Choice: Bummer or Woohoo

Each day is a series of good and bad things. When something bad happens, I say, "Bummer." When something good happens, I say, "Woohoo!" As I go through my day, I'll run into both bummers and woohoos. It's not a matter of adding them up and balancing them; it's a matter of letting the bummers go and celebrating the woohoos. You can say these in your mind—like when a beautiful woman sits next to me on the plane, I think, but don't yell, "WOOHOO!" At least not any more.

In my near-perfect job as a professional speaker, I travel a lot.

A typical day starts by driving to the airport. Some days, the parking attendants tell all drivers to park in a lot that's a ten-minute drive from the terminal. For me, that's a "little" bummer. However, for the guy in the car next to me, I've seen it become a HUGE problem as I watch him hit his hands on the dash and yell. The security people have nothing to do until someone like him comes along . . . and suddenly, they're swarming around him. What does he expect as an outcome of his bizarre tantrum? Does he think security will say, "Oh, you're distraught. Why don't you park right in front?" No! They're on him like a cheap suit. It's a bummer to move his car, but he experiences a *major* bummer as they strip him and his car down to the frame!

We park in the remote lot, then take a shuttle to the terminal. Once we get there, we have to go through security, which takes *two* hours. And that's a what? Sorry, wrong, that's not a bummer to me; it's a woohoo to me—because it didn't take *three* hours! When I arrive at the gate and stand in line to try to score a free upgrade to first class, I hear the flight is delayed due to mechanical problems. For me, that's just another "bummer," but for the guy in front of me (who doesn't have a Comic Vision), he screams at the gate agent, "I don't care if the plane is broken! I have to go to Boston!" And he stalks off. I walk up and say, "I have a different opinion . . . If the plane is broken, I'm not getting on. And quite frankly, you can't make me." The agent laughs and says, "You made me laugh. I'm going to upgrade you to first class." What's that? A woohoo!

Ten minutes later, they cancel the flight. Bummer. I eventually land in Boston on time to do my program. Woohoo!

Situational Stress Factors

One of the first steps to developing a Comic Vision is to identify the situational stress factors, then actively avoid them or insulate yourself from them.

For example, several years ago, I spoke for a group of welfare fraud investigators—600 of the angriest people I've ever met. About halfway through the program, one of the guys stood up and crossed his arms. I asked him, "What causes you stress?" He blurted out, "She lied to me!" I said, "Duh. It's fraud . . . What did you think would happen when you took this job? If you're a fraud investigator, aren't people going to lie? Yes!" I explained that *this is job security* and not a "bad thing." It's like real estate agents being angry that people keep calling to buy property. Duh.

Instead of complaining, I believe in finding a Comic Vision to get past the stress. Preparing to speak for the fraud investigators, my research showed that a major frustration for them was arresting people but never seeing them end up in jail. To employ Comic Vision to overcome this problem, I found a special desk "prop"—novelty sunglasses made of two forks welded together. The tines became the lenses and the handles became the earpieces. When they put on these glasses and tilted their heads sideways, they could see what these people looked like behind bars . . . just one time. Of course, they wouldn't wear these glasses at work, but just seeing them nearby on their desks helped them use their Comic Vision to see stressors and let them go!

Toxic People and Psychic Vampires

Some "employee tourists" fight situational stress factors until they finally leave. They bring their baggage to work and, as you know, that can be negative no matter what happens. They seem to delight in "sharing" their negativity, infecting the rest of us with their toxic thoughts.

I refer to these toxic people as psychic vampires. *Beware of them.* Like vampires, they feed on you—sucking the life right out of your throat. No matter what good thing happens, they find something bad. I saw a guy on TV who'd just won $18 million in the state lottery and didn't appear at all happy. In fact, he stood, arms crossed, and stared ahead as if he were angry. (If I won Powerball, I'd tell you to look in the dictionary under yippy-skippy-happy. It would say, "see Tim Gard.") When asked about his winning $18 million, this guy actually *complained* and said, "Now I have to pay $6 million in taxes." Yikes. I live for the day I have to pay $6 million in taxes.

Take traffic as another example. If you live in Los Angeles, you don't drive on the freeways at 5:00 p.m. and agonize, "*Who* are these people and *why* are they all driving at the same time?" If you can't deal with traffic, move to Anchorage, Alaska. I was in Anchorage recently, listening to the radio and turned up the volume to hear the announcer say, "And now the traffic report: There's a car . . . yup, there's another one . . ."

Humor Rituals

Develop a Comic Vision so you can leave work at work and home at home. Start the day with a Comic Vision good humor ritual and do the same when leaving at night.

A lot of people pile up their work problems, put them on a chair, and wheel them out, dragging them all the way home. When they get home and talk about their day, they point to the bundle of problems on the chair and say, "There's my day. Deal with *that* day!" Then they wheel that bundle back to work the next morning.

If that's what you do, at the end of every day from now on, do your dismount from your chair, command it to stay put, then point your finger at it and, like you'd tell a dog, say, "Stay." Then leave it behind.

Again, having a Comic Vision isn't about telling jokes. *It's about recognizing that everybody goes through this.* At the start of the day, get a good laugh by reading Joke-of-the-Day or Far Side. At the end of each day, take your phone and turn it upside down—or pick another humor ritual that signifies, "I'm done for now."

Learn to enjoy whatever comes your way by following these three rules.

Rule #1: Have Fun

I have fun wherever I go and, frankly, nobody's going to stop me. That goes for when I travel. If you travel on planes as often as I do, you know the airlines lose luggage. I own a common suitcase that has one distinction—mine is the only one with orange chicken feet sticking out. When it's in the overhead, nobody messes with my bag. And when the airline loses it, the entire staff gets a good laugh when I retrieve it.

When someone claims a lost bag, the attendant tosses the traveler a laminated card to pick out the color, model, and size. I tell them I don't need that card because I have a distinctive bag—a black carry-on roller bag. The guy indignantly retorts, "We have *hundreds* of bags like that." I explain, "Mine has orange chicken feet sticking out of it." Deflated, he quietly says, "It's right here." Then he yells, "The chicken feet guy is here!" They all come running out.

I have fun with security. A guy reaches in my bag and pulls out the rubber chicken. He seriously frisks it, pats it down, hands it back to me, and says, "It's clear, sir." What does he expect me to say? I ask, "Were you looking for the nuggets?" If the airlines are going to search my bag or lose my bag, we're all going to have a good laugh.

Rule #2: Do It For Yourself

First and foremost, Comic Vision is for *your* enjoyment. You do so many things for so many people that if you don't have fun for yourself, you can't inspire others to have fun either. I check into hotels 200 days a year. Often when I arrive late at night, they've given away my nonsmoking room. I don't smoke but they try to put me in a smoking room, which I don't like.

I used to walk up to the counter expecting trouble. But after I learned that most hotels have nonsmoking *suites*, I'd ask for a free upgrade to a nonsmoking suite. They'd routinely tell me, "Our *policy* doesn't allow upgrades based on smoking preference." To insulate myself from this, I started writing my own policy book about ten years ago. While at the counter, I reach in my bag and pull out *my* official-looking policy manual. On the cover, it says in big block letters, "These are the policies of Tim Gard and Comic Visions." I turn to the section on hotel policy, find the specific policy that applies (2001-10.5), then read it. "My policy clearly states: 'If Tim Gard requests and reserves a nonsmoking room at any hotel and that hotel gives his nonsmoking room away prior to his arrival, then that hotel is required, by law, to provide Tim Gard with an upgrade to a nonsmoking suite *at no additional cost.*' . . . It's my policy." The desk clerk replies, "Well, that's not *our* policy. You need to talk to the manager." I respond, "Unfortunately, my number one policy is: I don't repeat my policies. Once I've said the policy, I'm forbidden to talk about it any more. I'd like to help you, but . . . it's a policy." He repeats, "Sir, it's not *our* policy." Then I ask him to show me the hotel's policy manual. He tells me management doesn't have one. "Weeelll, I think we're going to have to go with *my* policy on that," I declare. So after displaying my policy manual, I do get upgraded with little agitation.

This tactic doesn't always work, but at the least, we both have fun and it's helped me change my attitude when I come in late. I walk in expecting fun rather than trouble. That's where Comic Vision comes in.

Rule #3: Share the Laughter

In my Comic Vision seminars, I use visual reminders to help audience members take their Comic Visions back to the office and share them with others. I love using ordinary items in extraordinary ways and extraordinary items in ordinary ways to resolve situational stressors. It's simple: Identify one stressor at a time, then search for a Comic Vision toy or prop to help deal with it.

Here's how one of Tim's Toys worked perfectly. My former boss would frequently leave the department without putting anybody in charge—he said he didn't want to play favorites. When people would come into my office and demand to see my supervisor, I'd have to say: "I don't know who that is today. I want to know, but . . . come back tomorrow. I think we'll know then."

After that happened lots of times, the employees took charge and got the Crown of Power—a full-sized, gold-colored plastic crown with fake jewels. We'd put someone in charge of our department for the day and that person would wear the toy crown. When it was my turn and someone said, "I want to talk to the top person," I'd come out wearing the Crown of Power, saying, "I'm the king; may I help you?" We laughed a lot. If someone in your office has a problem with authority or leadership, this may be just the solution.

Having trouble with computers? Whenever the system crashed where I used to work, one of the computer guys would snort, "What have you done to the system?" So I got these soft voodoo dolls that look like a miniature computer monitor and keyboard. When he'd ask, "What have you done?" I'd say, "Nothing," then jab at the voodoo doll with a large pin. Just by sitting on your desk, props like the voodoo-doll computer can make the difference between being irritated . . . or being reminded to see the humor.

The Comic Vision Oath

Comic Vision is a matter of timing—turning around whatever bothers you whenever you can. Please promise me this: that from now on, you'll take the Comic Vision "oath" and use laughter to create a more perfect job.

Raise your right hand and repeat: "I, (state your name), promise to use my Comic Vision every day. I will not carry broken glass in my pocket. I'll have fun. I'll do it first for myself and I'll share it." Now you have a Comic Vision. If you use your Comic Vision, then you will act, not react, to situational stress.

Now go do that voodoo you do so well, be the best you can be, and use your Comic Vision to overcome the situational stress factors you face every day.

In Review

Have Fun

Do It For Yourself

Share the Laughter

About the Author

Tim Gard, CSP

Tim is fall-out-of-your-seat, tears-in-your-eyes, laugh-out-loud funny! He's an outrageous speaker who uses props and brilliant timing to weave stories and playful moments into his presentations.

His interactive Comic Visions program gets people to adopt strategies that harness laughter in their lives. As a result, they learn to see the world through their own Comic Visions. Tim's Toys (his fun and funny props) serve as visual reminders to act on—not react to—life's stressful moments. These props can be seen and purchased at *www.timgard.com* to help lighten up your office place and life in general.

From Singapore to Sioux City, Tim has been "cracking 'em up" as a professional speaker since 1984. As he says, "Remember, laughter becomes you."

Contact Information:

Tim Gard, CSP
Comic Visions LLC
4150 Ireland St.
Denver, CO 80249

Phone: 800-865-9939 • Fax: 303-932-0990
www.timgard.com • E-mail: Tim@TimGard.com

Dying for a Good Laugh

How to keep your sense of humor through grief and loss

by Ronald P. Culberson, MSW, CSP

You cannot keep the birds of sorrow from flying over your head, but you can keep them from building nests in your hair. – Chinese proverb

Death is fascinating. I don't particularly enjoy it, but I'm fascinated by the way people in our society tend to act like it will go away if they ignore it. When people die, we whisk them off to the funeral home where they are out of sight. We bury them in new cemeteries where the ground level tombstones don't show. And we refer to those unfortunate people by saying they have "departed," "passed away," or "expired" rather than admitting they have simply "died!"

When I went to work as a social worker in hospice care, I expected to find this attitude in place. However, I was pleasantly surprised to find people who openly discussed death, and patients who continually inspired me with their courage and strength. Don't get me wrong. I still met the same resistance in the real world. At most social gatherings, I would explain my career and get one of two responses. People would either say, "You must be a very special person," or they'd just walk away. I don't consider myself special but I do find that my experiences show some of the most gallant uses of humor—in the face of death and loss.

Visiting Mary

In the fall of 1987, while working as a home care social worker for Hospice of Northern Virginia, I met an extraordinary patient named Mary. I had visited Mary in her home and, although she was very ill, she was doing relatively well and had the support of a loving family. Two weeks later, however, she took a turn for the worse and was transferred to the hospice inpatient facility. I went to see her the day she arrived there.

The moment I walked into Mary's hospice room, I realized her situation had changed dramatically. The color in her face was gone. Her listless body sank into the mattress as though she had no strength.

As I approached, a look of recognition warmed her face. I took her frail hand in mine and asked, "How are you doing?"

"Not good," she whispered.

"Are you getting what you need?"

"Oh, they're spoiling me," she said with a weak grin. "The nurses have been so nice—they seem to anticipate my every need."

Then Mary rose up on her elbows, took a look around the room, and announced, "This place is beautiful. I had heard so much about it, *I was dying to see it*!" I froze, not knowing how to respond.

Mary closed her eyes, fell back on her pillow, and let loose a burst of laughter.

"Can you believe I said that?" she bubbled. We laughed together while I marveled at her brave use of humor in the face of such daunting circumstances.

Six hours later, Mary died.

Mary had "it"—a special balance that allowed her to see both the seriousness of her situation *and* the humor in it. She knew she was dying, yet allowed herself to enjoy a moment of fun. She saw the humor when others would have been afraid to acknowledge it. Or they'd have been so overwhelmed by the magnitude of the adversity, they wouldn't have been able to see it.

Getting Back to Being Serious

Irish-born playwright and author George Bernard Shaw said, "Life does not cease to be funny when people die, just as it does not cease to be serious when people laugh." Most of us cannot live out this truth in life, much less in death. We continue to say things like "I have to stop goofing off and get back to work," but we never say "I have to stop working and get back to goofing off!" A break from the seriousness of our lives can be just what we need to rejuvenate ourselves.

When we face grief and loss, we may believe there is no place for humor, that humor is offensive, disrespectful, or inappropriate. However, if used sensitively, humor can be a wonderful way, not only to cope, but also to balance the tragedies in our lives. Winston Churchill said, "It is my belief you cannot deal with the most serious things in the world unless you understand the most amusing." Humor is about the balance that exists in real life: joy and tragedy. We must experience both to truly appreciate the richness life has to offer.

Here are suggestions on how to use three FUNdamental benefits of humor to make life's unbearable moments better. They allow us to die laughing!

FUNdamental 1: Use humor to provide a BALANCE to stress.

In her book *Making Sense of Humor*, Lila Green said, "Time

flies whether you're having fun or not." So far, we have a money-back guarantee that we will die. Realizing the end result, there is a wonderful argument for adding fun to our lives. Even in times of grief and loss, we can make this process more bearable by infusing humor.

The days following my seven-year-old nephew's death were a blur of activities. The busyness of making funeral arrangements, greeting friends, and sharing memories kept us conveniently distracted so that we wouldn't stumble into the pockets of grief scattered throughout our minds. We knew we'd spend enough time there in the months ahead, so we welcomed these distractions.

After two viewings, a memorial service, and a graveside service, our family gathered at my parents' home for a needed meal and some rest. We picked at our dinner, the generously donated gifts of the usuals: casseroles, homemade rolls, and brownies. Then we slumped into our seats in the living room and let out a collective sigh. We looked like warriors who had just returned from battle, our faces showing the fatigue of defeat. Then, for the next two hours, we told jokes.

In retrospect, this seems crazy. It even hints of disrespect, yet no one protested. Was it disrespectful? Was it wrong? Were we teetering on the edge of sanity? Not at all. We were feeling the effects of grief overload and needed a break. Not a break that was disrespectful or cruel, but a healing break that would allow us to face our grief the next morning with renewed strength. We knew the days ahead would be full of feelings from the loss we'd experienced, but in that moment in my parents' living room, the laughter gave us the strength to go on.

At the comedian Henny Youngman's funeral, the rabbi leading the service said, "God, take Henny Youngman . . . please." This was a callback to the line Youngman used in much of his comedy routine, "Take my wife . . . please." It brilliantly captured the essence of both Henny Youngman's career and his death. Neither disrespectful nor silly, the humor allowed participants to experience an escape from the heaviness of the service.

In hospice and palliative care, the focus is on quality of life, not quantity. Hospice workers often refer to the "*life* in your *days*" rather than the "*days* in your *life*." This captures the essence of the balance that humor offers. It's vital if we're going to get to the end of our lives with a sense of satisfaction and accomplishment.

At the hospice where I worked, a volunteer named Kathy always searched the obituaries to find individuals who had designated our hospice as the recipient of donations. She would pass these on to our staff so that proper acknowledgments could be made to donating families. But Kathy also searched for funny obituaries that she'd pass on to me!

One obituary said that a man had "gone to be with Jesus in his home in Palmyra." I'm surprised this announcement didn't cause a sudden hoard of bus tours to the "new" holy land in Palmyra!

Another appeared on April 14 but said that the woman died in her sleep on "April 17." We thought we should warn her!

My favorite was about a woman described this way: "She was known for her graciousness and sense of humor. Toward the end, her respirations assisted but breathing with difficulty, she said, 'Is there any oxygen loose in the room that I'm not getting? Perhaps there is some trapped in the bedclothes!'" How great is that? A woman who is near death but can still share a bit of humor. This is a gift with which we should all be blessed.

FUNdamental 2: Use humor to CONNECT with others.

Going through loss is such an isolating experience. We feel disconnected from the living world because we're experiencing this lonely sense of grief. We turn to humor as a powerful way to connect with others, thus keeping us from feeling even more isolated.

After giving a presentation to the American Cancer Society, I was approached by a woman who said, "I have to tell you what happened to me." She explained that while she was going through her own cancer treatment—not a particularly funny experience, mind you—she lost all her hair. Though she wasn't embarrassed by her bald head, she could tell that others were. So, on most days, she wore a scarf to cover it.

When invited to a Halloween costume party, she couldn't decide on a costume that worked well with her scarf. So she painted her head black and then painted a giant white "8" on the back of her head! Yes, she went as one of those magic eight balls that uses the floating triangle to answer your ponderous questions with ridiculously mysterious answers like "Maybe yes" or "It's possible." Then, on several pieces of paper, she wrote out "answers," put tape on the back, and kept them in her hand. All night long, she would go up to people and say, "Ask me a question." When they'd ask her a question, she'd shake her head and slap an answer on her forehead. Although her bald head had been a barrier to others, she turned a disadvantage into a distinct advantage by allowing others to laugh with her about her unusual "head" case.

One day, while visiting a hospice patient Mr. Smith, I walked into his bedroom and asked my typical introductory question, "How are you feeling today?" Considering that I worked with terminally ill people, that question might seem a bit odd. Nonetheless, it always got the conversation started. Mr. Smith responded, "I feel like I have one foot in the grave and the other on a banana peel!"

As a hospice patient, the fact that Mr. Smith just made a humorous reference to death was uncommon. In fact, it was so uncommon, I was sure it wasn't intended to be humorous. Risking a blatant misinterpretation, I said, "That's funny."

"I know," Mr. Smith replied. "I used to be the jokester in my family. I was always sharing jokes at dinner, bringing home funny movies, and generally just joking around. Ever since I've been sick, my family treats me as if I'm already dead."

Later during that visit, I asked Mr. Smith's family to join us and took a moment to explain his perspective. They had no idea how he felt about humor and regretted how the intensity of their emotions had prevented them from realizing this. That day, they vowed to change the situation. I found out later that they rented five comedy videos and watched them together over the next few days. From that point on, humor was going to be a part of *their* lives—and *his* death.

I saw Mr. Smith a few weeks after that visit and, though his illness had progressed, he looked very much alive. His family had given him back his soul; the humor had reconnected them all.

Fundamental 3: Use humor to see a new PERSPECTIVE.

The problem with adversity, especially death, is that we tend to only see one perspective—a negative one. The nature of humor, however, is that it creates a new perspective. In fact, a joke take us down one contextual path and then changes directions. It's this new perspective that makes us laugh!

Here's an example. A three-legged dog walked into an old west saloon and said, "I'm looking for the man who shot my paw." Some of you will get that later! You see, the word paw takes on two meanings (pa for father and paw for foot) and it is those two meanings that make the joke funny...for some of us!

In Kirk Douglas's book *A Stroke of Luck*, Douglas describes his experiences after having a stroke. Feeling frustrated during the rehabilitation process, he considered suicide and actually had a loaded gun in his mouth – until it bumped against a sore tooth. He reacted with laughter because he realized that a sore tooth had delayed his suicide! The experience prevented him from following through and he realized the importance humor had played in the process.

Kirk Douglas knew that humor led him to a new perspective. It allowed him to see the absurdity in an otherwise desperate situation. Once he had changed his viewpoint, he found new energy with which to cope.

Viktor Frankl survived the atrocities of concentration camps in World War II. While in Auschwitz and two other camps, he realized he needed to view his circumstances in a way that would lead to survival, not death. While many other prisoners gave up and died, he was determined to live. By hoping for a better outcome and finding humor in the most unusual circumstances, Frankl discovered that "the last of the human freedoms is to choose one's attitude in any given set of circumstances." He knew that his perspective was the key to his survival. In fact, he became so good at seeing the humor in the day-to-day tragedies of that environment, he trained a fellow prisoner to find one funny story each day.

Someone once said, "There is nothing wrong with getting older. It's when you stop getting older that the trouble starts." Whether telling jokes to balance stress, sharing humor to connect us with loved ones, or using the power of humor to create a new perspective, humor helps us maneuver the most challenging time in our lives—our deaths.

We can't determine what happens to us in this world but we can determine how we respond. If we allow ourselves to embrace humor as a way to respond to the joyful *and* tragic times in life, our lives will be rich and balanced. As author Robert Louis Stevenson said, "The man is a success who has lived well, laughed often and loved much."

In Review

Use humor to provide a BALANCE to stress.

Use Humor to CONNECT with others.

Use Humor to see a new PERSPECTIVE.

About the Author

Ronald P. Culberson, MSW, CSP

Ron, who is Director of Everything! at FUNsulting, etc., helps people have more FUN while preserving the integrity of the work they do and the lives they lead. He works with organizations that want their people to use humor to manage stress and be more effective.

An experienced hospice social worker, a senior manager, and a 20-year researcher of the benefits of humor, Ron has provided FUN presentations to 50,000+ people in more than 500 corporations, associations, government agencies, and non-profit organizations.

Contact Information:

Ronald P. Culberson, MSW, CSP
Director of Everything!
FUNsulting, etc.
665 Old Hunt Way
Herndon, VA 20170

Phone: 703-742-8812
Fax: 703-318-1431
www.FUNsulting.com
E-mail: Ron@FUNsulting.com

Phone Fun For Fabulous Financial Success

By June Cline, CSP

"**D**on't hang up! Please don't hang up. And, please don't cuss me, Ms. Cline. I've been cussed at all day. I know it's Christmas Eve, Ms. Cline, but I gotta eat, too. This will only take a minute of your time. Okay, Ms. Cline?"

I began to laugh. High humor it wasn't. But how could I hang up on someone who had just asked me not to "cuss" him? "What's your name?" I asked. With that question, I was engaged. I didn't hang up and I didn't cuss him. I wanted to know who he was.

Today, I can't remember what he was selling, but I do remember Derrick. I remember his different and funny approach to get me to stay on the line. That's what using just a "titch" of humor on the phone can do for you — get them to engage. It's the oldest sales trick in the book — to build rapport with your client or prospect ASAP. And it has to happen quickly.

Derrick probably didn't know he had followed one of the biggest rules and best-kept secrets in comedy. For more punch for his comedic buck, he used a "k"- sounding word —"cuss." Words like crackers, cookies, kittens, bike, kiss, kid are all in the "k"-sounding family. Although no one truly knows why this works, the theory is that when we were kids, we were "picked" up and "cuddled" and "kissed" and given "candy" and "cookies" and told that we were "cute." As babies, we internalized the "k" sound and actually began to connect the hard consonant sound with all the good feelings that surround it — the good stuff that makes us smile.

Comedic Wit

What Derrick — a great "k"-sounding name — didn't know is that for even more bang for his comedic buck, he should have placed the hard consonant strategically at the end of the sentence. And, though this is the case with my great "k"-sounding name as well, it's much more effective if the "punch" word is the last sound heard.

If Derrick had known this, he could have said, "Don't hang up! Please don't hang up. And, please, Ms. Cline, don't cuss me!" Cuss is the surprise word, the punch word. The theory here is for the last hard consonant sound to roll around in the ol' noodle. It allows us to take our own special comedy trip down memory lane, reviving all those good feelings from babyhood.

To give others some much-needed phone fun, use the following Phone Fun Tips to help you add humor to your conversations. This will give you an edge — that "something extra" — to help your prospects, clients, and, yes, even family and friends think about *you* when they need what you have to offer. Just like Derrick. He made me laugh and I'm still talking about him years later.

Phone Fun Tip #1: Want to!

You "gotta wanna." Do you value humor? Or do you believe it's a frivolous waste of a taxpayer's money? I have been in companies in which laughter was "forbidden" on the sales floor. Seriously, folks, how somber must we be about kitty litter? Realize that humor is a value-added part of the sales process. It doesn't replace product knowledge, doing your homework, or honing selling skills. It merely means people are less likely to slam down the phone cussin' if you are entertaining, interesting, or having fun on the phone — just like I was with Derrick. "Want to" reflects your attitude about using humor, which determines whether you will or you won't use it. And you know what they say about not using it.

Phone Fun Tip #2: Listen for Laughter

Listen for "natural" laughter in your conversation. Just by shifting your attention to noticing laughter, you'll be amazed at how laughter-filled your conversations already are.

I invite you to take a closer, more analytical look at the process. Who initiates the laughter over the phone? Become aware of the number of times you (or your prospect or client) instigate laughter and on what topics. Make note of those topics to help you be on the lookout for more humor in those areas. Actually count the number of laughs by making a tic mark every time laughter is generated. Set up a "T" bar labeled "Me/Them" and become aware of who is the comedic instigator.

Why is this important? Because he who instigates laughter wins. He wins recognition, respect, and reward. According to a friend of mine, a former nurse now turned humorist, "laughter increases the 'receive-ability' of endorphins"— nature's wonder drug. If you instigate the laugh, you make others feel good. You actually change their brain chemistry; you change their state of mind. They begin to associate you with the laughter and that feel-good feeling. They like you more and they don't even know why.

And don't we all love to buy from and associate with people we like? In a study by the American Trade Association, 74% of the respondents said, all things being equal in products and services, they would change the companies they did business with in order to have more fun. With the weight of today's complex world on our shoulders, "laughter equals hope" (to quote myself). If you aren't instigating humor, you are "the weakest link. Goodbye!" As the great comedy writer and humorist Melvin Helitzer once told me, "Keep up the good humor work, kid. The world needs us." I believe that's true now, more than ever.

Phone Fun Tip #3: Prepare to Banter

Many of us are good at verbal sparring with friends. Many more of us are a "titch" uncertain about trying it with prospects and clients. And yet, it can be one of the quickest, easiest, and biggest connectors—a sign of good rapport-building. For me, it also indicates if I want to do business with certain people. I believe life's too dang short to work with a cantankerous person. (Ain't "cantankerous" a *great* "k" word x 2!)

Here's an example of quick rapport-building on the phone. I had met a prospect at an association conference meeting. After a nice first-meeting conversation, I told him I would contact him the following week. When the conference was over, I decided to stop in a fast food place for lunch before I hit the road on my five-hour trip home. To my surprise, there sat the gentleman from the conference with whom I had just bonded. Not wanting to ignore him or be rude, I walked up to his table and said, "Hi, may I join you?" "Sure," he replied, and motioned for me to sit down. As I put my tray down on his table, I saw his construction-worker boots and realized he was *not* the man from the conference. I quickly tried to remove myself by saying, "I'm sorry. You're not who I thought you were." "Well, Ma'am," he said, "I was just wonderin' who you was." I apologized again, my face glowing like a neon sign in a brothel (not that I know what that looks like). He then *insisted* I join him. I was so embarrassed that I just sat down —which was okay, until Joe's other construction buddies came piling in for lunch, too. Between their comments to Joe about his "menu selection," and the ever-growing number of men staring at me—well, let me just say I set a new definition for the term "fast food." I was outta there!

Flash forward to the next week and my phone conversation to set up my meeting with the real guy. "Hi, this is June Cline; I met you at the conference." "Yes, I remember," he replied. "You got me in so much trouble!" I exclaimed. This quiet, reserved businessman was in stunned silence for a moment before asking, "How did I do that?" "Well, I had lunch with you ... and . . . you weren't there," I replied.

He burst out laughing as I told him the story. We proceeded to set up our business meeting and by then we were well on our way to building a great relationship. My "idiot moment," as I call it, turned a routine sales call into a fun, upbeat business meeting, which led to more than a million dollars in sales. And, like Derrick, I could call that man today and say, "Hi, remember me?" I bet a million comedic bucks that he would. Good ol' Joe and the boys probably remember me, too. And that's the point. They'll remember you—if you make 'em laugh.

Phone Fun Tip #4: Play with Words and Topics

You've already been introduced to one of my favorite made-up units of measurement—a "titch." It's bigger than a smidgen but less than a skosh. I luv to play with words. In my speeches and sales presentations, I always use words that are unique to me—a made-up hybrid of one or more words or sayings. I affectionately call these my "Junie-isms."

I'm amazed at the number of people who remember them and begin to use them. They come back to me after my presentation in e-mails or phone messages in a playful manner, such as "Wish we'd had a 'titch' more time with you."

I'm also amazed at the number of people who comment about my voice mail phone message: "Hi, you have *almost* reached June Cline. I help people learn how to 'Lead, Laugh... or Get Out of the Way!' And, I am just not available right now. If you will leave your name and number, I'll be 'tickled to life' to call you back." People have booked me for speaking engagements strictly off of this voice mail message. They said they "loved the energy, enthusiasm, and creativity" in my voice mail message. Some have told others to call my number just to hear this fun message. So that's what all those hang-ups are!

"Tickled to life" is one of my Junie-isms. Being "tickled to death" has never appealed to me. In my research, I've never been able to track the origin of the phrase. My theory is that "tickled to death" comes from the death-like body language reactions we have when we experience "knee-slapping" laughter.

Think about it. Our mouths are usually wide open, slack, agape. We can't breathe, or we gasp for air. Some of us look like rigor mortis has set in as we go into convulsion-like spasms. We laugh so hard we cry. (Funny, I realize I have just described a dance partner or two in this same condition. But, I digress.)

"Lead, Laugh or Get Out of The Way" is the title of my flagship communication program. It, too, is a play "with" words from the famous quote, "Lead, follow, or get out of the way." People love it—they get it—they repeat it.

So play with some of your favorite phrases to come up with something uniquely "you" that others will want to repeat. They will remember you. And for that, you'll be "tickled to life!"

Phone Fun Tip #5: Seek Professional Help

It's okay to seek professional help. Heck, we all need it from time to time. If you are serious about using humor in your life and sales arsenal, you may want to engage the expertise of a professional humor coach. Several are found right in this anthology.

Being humorous on the phone isn't as easy as it looks. There are many rules and tribulations—not to mention timing—which becomes a totally different animal when on the phone than in person. You can't see facial expressions or body language to know if you are truly connecting with the other person. You have to *feel* it. So, yeah, it's risky.

This is the perfect place to throw in the disclaimer, "If in doubt, leave it out." It's not worth losing a valued customer by over-stepping someone's boundaries, all in the name of phone fun. However, the boundary line is way out there for some people. And, truly, the essence of humor is to push the edge of that way-out envelope.

My First Humor Coach

I'll never forget my first call to a humor coach. I'd heard about him through the National Speakers Association (NSA), of which we both were, and still are, members. I had come to his town on business and gathered up the courage to call him. I said, "Hi, you don't know me and I don't know you but

I understand you are a comedy coach and I would like to buy you lunch." L-O-N-G pause. "Well," he said, "what do ya look like?" With a titch shorter pause, I replied, "You understand, kind sir, this call is not of a sex-u-al nature." What made this funny was exaggerating my heaviest southern, Scarlett O'Hara drawl. We both laughed and he replied, "Unfortunately, they never are!" A coach and a new friend were born that day.

T. Bubba Bechtol, of Grand Ol' Opry fame, gave me validation and encouragement that my style and humor manner were congruent with who I am. Sometimes we just need someone else to tell us it's working, it's funny, and we can do it.

Flash forward a few years — and several coaches — later. My phone rings and it's Bubba. He's heard that I have yet one more humor coach. "June, Bubba. How many coaches ya had, girl?" "I don't know, Bubba, a few. Why?" "June, you are turning into a 'Coach Ho.' It's time to have confidence in yourself and just get out there and do it."

Those words of wisdom from Bubba are so true. You can learn *about* it for the rest of your life (and I intend to because I love it so), but at some point, as Bubba said, "Ya just gotta do it."

Most Underused Tool on the Planet

Know that using humor is one of the most powerful and

underused tools on the planet. And it is one of the most prized and cherished gifts we can give the receiver. People are desperate to laugh and to lighten up. You can help make that happen by remembering the five phone fun tips: 1) want to, 2) listen for laughter, 3) prepare to banter, 4) play with words and topics, and 5) seek professional help.

You'll be well on the way to creating a fun phone experience for your clients, prospects, family, and friends. Just doing that will bring you recognition, respect, and reward. And, like Derrick taught me, they will rarely hang up on you or give you a cussin'. That's what happens when you lead the way to laughter, one of the most powerful selling tools on the planet. Because after all—we all gotta eat!

Phone Fun Tips

1. **Want to**

2. **Listen for Laughter**

3. **Prepare to Banter**

4. **Play With Words and Topics**

5. **Seek Professional Help**

About the Author

June Cline, CSP

June entertains and trains organizations that want their people to "Lead, Laugh . . . Or Get Out of The Way!" She is a Certified Speaking Professional through the National Speakers Association and a Distinguished Alumni of Westminster College of Salt Lake City, Utah.

Here are just a few comments from her happy clients: "Your humor is always refreshing and healing as we face our struggles in life. Our staff thoroughly enjoyed your presentation. You have always been special; thanks for facing the challenge to use your talents to the fullest." "You have a wonderful ability to educate and motivate."

Contact Information:

June Cline, CSP
Open Heart Communications
4101 East Baseline Rd.
Suite 1011
Gilbert, AZ 85234

Office: 480-634-7485
Fax: 480-361-9726
www.junecline.com
E-mail: june@junecline.com

Laughter– The Best Medicine?

by Brad Nieder, M.D.

Patients frequently come up to me and say, "Dr. Bruce, you always say, 'Laughter is the best medicine,' but listen to this: My sister's friend's second-cousin-once-removed's brother-in-law was drinking a beer last weekend, and the dog made him laugh so hard that he snorted the beer up his nose and ended up with a sinus infection. So, you see, doc, laughter ain't such a good medicine after all, is it?"

"My name's Brad," I reply.

My Hypothesis

But they got me thinking, those clever patients. Is laughter really the best medicine? Perhaps that common phrase isn't accurate at all. Perhaps laughter really is harmful to one's health. Some people claim to have laughed so hard they've been "in stitches." Others state they have been "weak in the knees" with laughter. Some folks even say they have "bust a gut" laughing. None of these is a desirable condition, but that last one would require an emergency laparotomy by a trauma surgeon. Certainly not good medicine!

I decided to investigate the theory. "Who's better qualified than I?" I thought. After all, I'm a trained physician and humorist, educated in the art of observing people naked without laughing, and armed with a white coat, safety goggles, and urinalysis cups. I can speak in acronyms such as: "We have a GSW with LOC. Start an IV. Draw a CBC with a PT and PTT. Get a UA and an ABG and call the ICU ASAP. Then SUV on over to the ATM so I can get a BLT while obtaining MP3s via DSL."

Testing the Hypothesis

Feeling eminently qualified, I set up a randomized, double blind, placebo-controlled study to test the hypothesis that laughter is the best medicine. After months of research and scrutiny, after tireless hours of experimentation and data analysis, after countless cups of coffee and Red Bull, I now can say, without reservation, that Percocet is the best medicine. In fact, laughter isn't even in the top three. Perhaps the popular phrase should be revised to read: "Laughter is the Best Medicine . . . unless you have an infection. Or you're having a heart attack, or you're recovering from surgery, or you have 'giggle incontinence.' So, laughter is about the fifth or sixth best medicine, but before embarking on any laughter regimen, please ask your doctor or pharmacist."

On the other hand, let's face it, laughter *is* very powerful. It's no secret. We've known the benefits of laughter for a long time. In fact, way back in the 17th century, a physician named Thomas Sydenham wrote, "The arrival of a good clown exercises more beneficial influence upon the health of a town than twenty asses laden with drugs."

Times have changed a little bit, because these days you can't call the pharmaceutical reps "asses." Not if you want to keep receiving free pens! I am kidding of course. "Asses" in this case means "donkeys." That's what they called them back then.

Well, Dr. Sydenham's statement got me thinking. So I now perform "Tickle Therapy" in my office. It's similar to shock therapy, but once I strap the patients down, I coat the soles of their feet with salt and then actually bring in donkeys to lick it off. Patients tell me they experience an amazing ticklish sensation. And the cure rate is apparently 100% because these patients never return for follow-up treatments.

Since Dr. Sydenham's day, numerous studies have been conducted to demonstrate the efficacy of laughter as a medicine. I haven't read these studies. I just don't have the attention span. I think it's a little ADD (Attention Deficit Disorder). It's no big deal. It's quite common actually. In fact, we all have a little ADD. A recent study in the *New England Journal of Medicine* stated that 80% of people with ADD have . . . Whoa! A smiling paperclip just knocked on my computer monitor at me! Hey guy! Nice eyebrows!

Read the Studies

Anyhoo, where was I? Oh, yes, medical studies. Even if I had the attention span, I just don't have the time, what with my busy schedule of keeping patients waiting for hours wearing backless paper dresses and browsing issues of *National Geographic* two decades old while I practice my putting. But I encourage you to read the studies. If you choose to do so, here are two pointers:

First, watch out for medical jargon. It's easy to get confused by all the scientific lingo. For example, check out the scientific definition of a laugh: "a psychophysiological reflex; a successive, rhythmic, spasmodic expiration with open glottis and vibration of the vocal cords, often accompanied by a baring of teeth and facial grimaces."

Oops, wait just a minute! That's actually the description of "rabies." Again, I am kidding. That really *is* the definition of a laugh. I'm trying to promote laughter as healthy, but the medical community makes it sound as pleasant as a vasectomy via tire iron.

Second, if you manage to wade through all the medical mumbo jumbo, make sure you review the studies with a critical eye. Sometimes there's a confounding factor in the methods used in the investigation. That's why so many studies seem to contradict each other. Eggs are good. No, eggs are bad. Well, margarine's good. No, margarine's bad. It's very confusing!

A recent report identified the foods that increase libido. (Ha! You were nodding off there, but now I have your attention again. Everyone wants to know how to increase sex drive!) Libido-boosting foods include romaine lettuce, celery, asparagus, onions, tomatoes, and sunflower seeds. In this case, it turns out if you read very carefully, you'll find that all the subjects used in this study were squirrels. And the control group—the group that did not have increased libido—consisted of the late Ernest Borgnine. So be careful drawing any conclusions from this study. But, if you're desperate, start eating a lot of salads. It couldn't hurt.

Beneficial Results

So, if you manage to review the *Annals of Long and Boring Articles*, the *Journal of Absurd Medical Minutiae,* and other fine compendia, you'll find the following benefits of laughter:

1. Laughter is free (a great benefit in today's age of seeking cost-effective treatments).

2. It's free of dyes and perfumes (not to mention free of artificial flavors and colors, fat-free, sugar-free, sodium-free, and cholesterol-free).

3. It enhances our resistance to illness by boosting the immune system.

4. It reduces levels of stress hormones such as cortisol in the blood.

5. It enhances pain management by raising pain thresholds.

6. It provides a good, quick aerobic workout for the heart and lungs.

7. It provides a workout for the abdomen, diaphragm, and facial muscles.

8. It doesn't require filling out time-consuming insurance claims.

9. It enhances romance. (After all, numerous surveys indicate that a sense of humor is the most desirable trait in a mate. Who needs asparagus?)

Second Opinion

I can tell you're still skeptical. If you want a "second opinion," let me refer you to a lady who was in the audience during one of my recent speaking engagements. She came up to me after the presentation, her hand trembling from the effects of Parkinson's disease, and said, "You see my hand, doctor? See how it shakes? Well, it stopped shaking when I was laughing at your jokes. Thank you for treating me!" Wow! Powerful stuff! And better than most pills. Even Percocet.

So you see, laughter is indeed good medicine. I hope that soon Aetna will begin to accept physician referrals to comedy clubs ("still a two-drink minimum in addition to your co-pay"), but even if we do see that day, laughter can't stand alone. It's no miracle cure. Rather, it's effective as an integral part of a well-balanced, healthy lifestyle.

With that thought in mind, here's some additional medical advice, offered in the form of a tribute to my true mentor and favorite doctor: Dr. Seuss.

Rx for Happy, Healthy Living

Just a few miles down Route 2.4,
That quirky old town is a shambles no more.
It once had a problem with decent health care.
The E.R. was packed – not a gurney to spare.

The Grinch needed Prozac for feeling dejected.
The Star-Bellied Sneeches' tattoos got infected.
The Cat in the Hat? Always needing CAT scans.
And Sam? Always there puking green eggs and ham.

The town's only doctor was really discouraged.
He thought and he thought and he mustered the courage
To make up a pledge for preventive-type care
That the townsfolk recited right in the town square:

"I will not eat a lot of sweets.
I will not overeat red meats.
I will not drink a lot of booze.
Instead plain water I will choose.
I'll keep my portions smaller-sized.
I'll limit salt and all things fried.
I'll keep my fats the good kind like in soy and nuts and beans;
Olive oil; fish like salmon, tuna and sardines.
Fruits and veggies, fiber and whole grains are really key.
I'll pop my daily calcium and aspirin, E and C.
I'll get my antioxidants. I'll eat my lycopenes.
I'll eat Omega-threes and flavonoids. Now what that means
Is: I will choose the darker colors for my meals and snacks,
Like spinach green and berries blue and tea both green and black.
I'll choose tomatoes, broccoli, garlic, red wine and I'll win.
(For purely social reasons I will never drink white zin.)"

Several weeks passed and the doctor observed 'em.
Folks lost some weight. Evidently they'd heard him.
Encouraged, he thought as he walked down the street
That people, quite simply, aren't just what they eat.
They also have bodies and spirits and minds,
And so he wrote down a new set of guidelines:

"If you're smokin', cokin', tokin'—must be jokin'! That's obscene!
It's like sunnin' buns and fun under the sun with no sunscreen.
And while I scream of screens I'm keen on all those screening tests,
Especially the ones for colon, prostate and your breasts.
Wash your hands and brush and floss and buckle up to go.
Wear a helmet on your head (including down below!).
Challenge both your mind and body: paint or stretch or read,
Change your oil, toil in the soil pulling weeds,
Write, go fly a kite or test your might or take a walk,
Swim or hit the gym or shake your limbs to '50s rock.

"Get some satisfaction interacting with each other,
Whether Horton, Yertle, Whos from Whoville or your mother.
Don't be late or break a date with mates, don't hate or lie.
Do say 'please' and 'thank you,' smile and look folks in the eye.
Surround yourself with loved ones; it's a healthy way to live.
Say 'I love you,' 'sorry,' hug and kiss, learn to forgive.

"Most of all, though, love yourself and to yourself be true,
Trust your gut (you've fed it well), take risks, enjoy the view.
Ups and downs abound. They're all around, those highs and lows.
Don't give up, slow down, show up, fall down, get up and go!
Be present. Don't dwell on the past (its glories or its sorrows).
Be prepared. Look forward to (but don't count on) tomorrow.
Don't worry. And be happy. Listen to your favorite songs.
Do your best and make mistakes then fix what you did wrong.
Learn to love the little things like cookies freshly baked,
A sunny day, a rainy day and every breath you take.

My final tip," he wrote, "for living happily ever after
Is: have a sense of humor; the best medicine is laughter."

And then when he finished, that doctor so rare,
He posted his words right there in the town square.
Again, he took notice the next several weeks
And saw folks were nicer when walking the streets.
He saw people exercise, leave larger tips.
Old folks took classes and went on nice trips.
Lovingly, husbands held hands with their wives.
In short, he saw folks celebrating their lives.

And so if you go out on Route 2.4
To that quirky old town that's a shambles no more
And find that old doctor and buy him a drink
And ask him of all his advice does he think
There's one real key that's the most beneficial,
He'll smile and he'll pause and he'll look quite official.
He'll say, "Drink red wine and when you're in a funk,
Just laugh. Folks around you will just think you're drunk."

©2003 Brad Nieder, M.D.

About the Author

Brad Nieder, M.D.
The Healthy Humorist™

Dr. Brad Nieder has successfully combined the seemingly disparate worlds of humor and health care. He has often been compared to the famous Patch Adams, as exemplified by this statement: "Compared to Patch Adams, Brad Nieder is not very famous."

As an undergraduate student at Stanford University, Brad was a founding member of the SIMPS comedy troupe. While a medical student at the University of Colorado, he frequently performed stand-up comedy. He then took his unique style to the Medical College of Virginia for his residency. Now a general practitioner in Denver, he travels throughout the country spreading his message that "Laughter is the Best Medicine."

Contact Information:

Brad Nieder, M.D.
The Healthy Humorist™
Denver, Colorado

Phone: 866-HUMOR-MD
(866-486-6763)
www.healthyhumorist.com
E-mail: drbrad@healthyhumorist.com
Your Rx for Happy, Healthy Living!™

Becoming Light♥Hearted

Managing Stress Through Humor

by Izzy Gesell, MS Ed, CSP

The *really* good news is that by bringing more humor into your life you will eliminate a good deal of the negative stress you now contend with.

The *practical* good news is that everyone has a sense of humor and everyone can increase the amount of humor, joy, and laughter that comes into his or her life.

The *cautionary* good news is that this process involves changing habits and requires some effort and patience.

Once Upon a Time . . .

I was on a small plane that flew into some heavy turbulence. The plane, and all the passengers in it, started bouncing through the air like a rock skipping over a pond. Every time the plane would hit a bump, I'd grip the sides of my seat, because I thought the plane was going to crash. Every time the flight smoothed out, I'd relax.

I happened to look across the aisle and there, sitting next to his mother, was a boy of maybe six or seven years old. Whenever the plane would hit a bump, I'd tense up and moan in fear. The same bump would cause the boy to raise his arms and shout, "Wheeeeeee."

When the turbulence eased and the plane flew smoothly, I'd relax but the boy became frustrated. I remember him looking at the ceiling of the plane where he'd heard the pilot's voice before, and in a pleading voice call out, "Do it again!"

The Power of Self Talk

I realized that this boy and I were having completely different responses to a situation in which we had *exactly* the same information. I was stressed and he wasn't! I was frightened for my life, and the kid thought he was on a roller coaster. I got angry at first, then became curious. I thought back to my college psychology class when I learned about the stimulus response theory, the one written as "S – R."

Now, if a stimulus leads to a particular response, I reasoned, why did this bumpy stimulus lead to completely different responses for the boy and for me? How can identical stimuli cause different responses? Aha! It must have something to do with that dash in the equation between the "S" and the "R." That dash represents the instantaneous moment in which we decide what a stimulus means to us; what our belief about the stimulus is going to be. It's where we talk to ourselves in order to understand what's going on.

In this instance, my self-talk about the flight determined it was dangerous. The kid's self-talk said it was fun. Bingo! I clearly understood that stress is rarely an event in itself; rather, it's our perception about the event that causes the stress! Stress is not a *fact;* it's a *feeling.*

Four Components of An Experience

The boy and I also differed in each of the four ways our bodies respond to stimuli. These four areas of response are mental, physical, emotional, and spiritual. In other words, we humans are creatures of mind, body, heart, and soul. And in each of these areas, the boy and I reacted differently, *even though we were responding to the same information.*

- Mentally, I was thinking, "This is scary." He was thinking, "This is fun!"

- Physically, I was tense and tight. The boy, on the other hand, was loose and relaxed.

- Emotionally, I was dealing with fear. He was connected to joy and happiness.

- Spiritually, I was unsure about what the future held or why I was here; my young fellow traveler was at one with his universe!

How Humor Helps Manage Stress

Humor influences each of these four areas of response. Simply put, by strengthening your sense of humor, you become better able to alter your responses to the stressors in your life as well as turn stressors into neutral events. Here's how humor works to strengthen mind, body, heart, and soul:

Mentally, humor allows you to see multiple points of view. A laugh is your body's recognition of another perspective. Having more than one perspective in any situation is the key to managing stress successfully.

This explains why children's observations are funny to adults. A child sees a situation from one point of view while an adult sees the same circumstance from a completely different perspective. Both realities are correct while also being different.

For example, a seven-year-old girl asks her mother why Daddy has to bring so much work home that he doesn't play with her anymore. The mother explains, "Honey, he doesn't have time to finish it during the day." The little girl thinks for a minute and says, "Why don't they put him into a slower group?"

Jokes also contain multiple perspectives. At its core, a joke is a story about a problem. Structurally, the punch line to the joke is the solution to the problem from a different point of view than the one presented at the beginning of the joke. The bigger the shift in perspective, the bigger the laugh. In fact, the more you exercise your sense of humor, the more mentally flexible you will become.

> **ACTION STEP:** Think of a joke you have heard. See if you can identify the shift in perspective. From whose point of view did the joke start? From whose did it end?

Physically, humor serves several functions. One is to release tension from the body. Tension is the physical manifestation of stress. It turns out that laughter and tension cannot exist in the body at the same time. Remember a time you were moving something really heavy and you started to laugh. Couldn't hold on to the heavy thing, could you? In fact, "nervous laughter" is one of the body's ways to rid itself of stress when crying or other ways are not available.

The connection between the human body and mind is well documented. Both your thoughts and your actions impact your emotions; consequently, you can successfully approach your stress either by changing your thinking or by doing something physical. You can yell, throw things, punch a pillow, or just start laughing out loud. All will serve to release tension from your body. The laughter, however, will cause your body to believe you are actually *happy*. This outcome releases different neuro-peptides and enzymes than when you feel angry, resentful, or scared. This physical state is more conducive to positive health than the physical states brought about by antagonism or frustration.

ACTION STEP: Practice laughing out loud for no reason other than to see how your body feels after doing it.

Emotionally, humor works by manipulating psychological distance and perspective. At times, it allows us to feel closer to people and events. At other times, it helps us gain distance and perspective on a situation. It, therefore, helps us both thrive and cope, restoring balance to our emotions.

Think about the people you most enjoy being with. Isn't their sense of humor an important factor in the quality of the relationship? I don't think any of us would consciously go into a personal relationship with someone who had no sense of humor. I'm not saying we won't end up in one like that, but we wouldn't choose that one if we could help it! The people we laugh with give our lives a sense of shared well-being. They are our energy-givers. For example, grandchildren and grandparents are energy-givers to each other.

Of course, we also have energy-drainers in our lives. They may be people we work with or perhaps even members of our family. They are the ones who, whether they call or come over, will suck the life force right out of us.

Spend as much time with energy-givers as possible and become an energy-giver to others by activating your sense of humor. I believe that shared laughter is love made audible. Shared laughter is a bond between people. It helps us feel connected to each other and less alone in this world.

Humor also protects against things that scare us or make us feel powerless. The advice to whistle a happy tune whenever we become afraid recognizes this function. Other examples are the concepts of "operating room humor" and "gallows humor" as evidenced in the movie "Life Is Beautiful" and the TV show "MASH." Whenever the world seems crazy, chaotic, or confused, humor helps us get through it.

ACTION STEP: Identify the energy-givers and energy-drainers in your life. Spend as much time as possible with energy-givers. Identify for whom you are an energy-giver.

Spiritually, humor is about "lifting our spirits"— taking ourselves lightly and recognizing that our physical reality is not the only one out there! A spiritual path is one upon which we pursue truth, meaning, and purpose in life. In a similar way, humor is always about someone's perception of truth, often about questioning what someone meant, and consistently finding new reasons to laugh about why we do what we do when we do it.

ACTION STEP: What does your sense of humor say about you and your view of the world and your place in it?

Expanding Your Sense of Humor

Here are five simple things to do that will help you develop your sense of humor. Do them regularly and they will become habits.

- **Be you own humor role model.** Find and display a picture of yourself smiling or laughing. Use it as a mirror.

- **Search for the happiness in others.** Make it your business to know what makes the people in your life happy. Your family, colleagues, office staff, and friends all enjoy something. Knowing what makes them laugh gives you an opportunity to plant seeds of pleasure in their lives. There is no greater morale builder than making others laugh. This technique will ensure that you are an energy-giver to others.

- **Find a humor buddy.** Pick someone who enjoys your sense of humor and whose humor you appreciate. Be in touch with that person on a regular basis, perhaps weekly. Together, either by phone, mail, or computer, share the humorous events of your lives: the funny things you overhear during the day, the marvelous web site you found, the headline in this morning's paper—see what I mean? Make it a great opportunity to contact that friend you've lost touch with over the years.

- **Set your mental channel to the humor in your life.** Most of the laughter and joy in life comes from everyday experiences. Slips of the tongue, puns, incongruities, overheard conversations, bureaucratic foul-ups, and silly personal mistakes make us laugh every day. By keeping track of what we find humorous, we can easily see how funny things occur all the time. Because we have not been trained to honor the humor in our lives, we generally allow it to come and go randomly.

  So hang on to the humor in your life it by writing down funny or incongruous incidents, cutting out cartoons and articles that make you laugh, collecting funny videos, greeting cards, and DVDs. This humor collection technique is what comedians and humorists use to gather the material that ends up in their acts.

- **Use your memory as a catalyst for humor.** Each day, keep handy a symbol or memento of something that has happy memories for you. Whenever you find yourself feeling stressed, take 15 seconds or so and focus on the memento. You will find yourself immersed in the positive feelings that the symbol represents. Use these joyful items to counteract the stressors. Stress management pioneer

Hans Selye believed that "nothing erases unpleasant thoughts more effectively than concentration on pleasant ones."

Let's say you have a book of matches from a trip you took to Paris ten years ago. You look at those matches and, in 15 seconds, your taste buds recall the meal, your ears hear the music, your nose sniffs the breeze that was wafting by, and a smile spreads across your heart.

Why does this work? Well, to your memory, an emotion is as real as the actual event. That's why you can look at a photograph of someone you love, and the love you feel is real.

Good news! You don't even have to buy a thing to use this technique! You have everything you need—perhaps in your basement, attic, or storage area. Those souvenirs and mementoes you've been collecting all your life now have a purpose!

Use this technique to help you detach from stressors you can't control. Focus on releasing tension in your body, then ask yourself, "What can I control in this situation?"

And The Winner Is? You!

Stress management begins with the realization that most of the stressors in our lives are predictable. We know who, what, and where our stressors are going to be well in advance of each day.

Since we can't always change the way the world works, our best shot at managing stress lies in our learning to "manage the dash"—to manage that interval between the event and our belief about that experience. We have a much better shot at changing our thinking about something than changing other people's behavior or altering things over which we have no control.

It's not that stress will disappear as you develop your humor skills. It's just that you will spend less time being stressed and more time being calm and smiling.

As Thomas Szasz observed, "In the animal kingdom, the rule is eat or be eaten; in the human kingdom, it is define or be defined." By actively expanding and strengthening our sense of humor, we are truly in the position of defining ourselves.

About the Author

Izzy Gesell, MS Ed, CSP

Izzy is a keynote speaker, professional facilitator, and presentation coach. The author of PLAYING ALONG: Group Learning Activities Borrowed From Improvisation Theater, Izzy is among the first speakers to bring the concepts of improv theater into business.

Originally from Brooklyn, New York (where a sense of humor is a survival skill), he has earned a BA in psychology, an MS in education, and a P (that's 1/3 of a Ph.D.). Nationally known as an expert in helping organizations and their people prosper during changing times, his clients include NASA, Microsoft, the National Wellness Conference, and the Texas Dental Association.

Contact Information:

Izzy Gesell, MS Ed, CSP
Head Honcho at Wide Angle Humor
PO Box 962
Northampton, MA 01061

Phone: 888-4GESELL
(888-443-7355)
www.izzyg.com
E-mail: izzy@izzyg.com

Humor, Hugs, and Hope

by Greg Risberg, CSP, MSW

On a bright Tuesday morning, I boarded a plane for the first leg of a four-day work trip to the East Coast, a journey crammed with back-to-back talks. We had just settled in our seats when we were told about a delay. Minutes later, we were asked to deplane because of "a possible mechanical problem."

I was anxious to get on with my trip, so my frustration escalated in the waiting area when an airline agent announced that our plane wouldn't be taking off at all—that the entire airport would be closed. No reason for this extraordinary development was given. I wandered to a restaurant just in time to see the horrifying footage of the World Trade Center terrorist attack that was destined to burn its image indelibly in our minds. I realized I wasn't going to be flying to the East Coast or giving any of my planned talks.

Driving home, I felt dazed and scared by the news reports of the escalating tragedy. Out of habit, I phoned in for my messages. There was a frantic call from a meeting planner in Peoria, Illinois—a three-hour drive from my home. His scheduled speaker was coming in from out-of-town and, like me, had been stranded. "Could you possibly make it to Peoria by car, and fill in for our speaker?" Sure, I could! I was all packed, my materials ready to go. I felt an overwhelming need to do *something*, to find a way to be useful. I could hardly say "yes" fast enough.

Once in Peoria, I asked the meeting planner what he thought people needed from a speaker that day. "We need to laugh and cry," he said, "and we need hope." The crying, I thought, would take care of itself: Could I help with the laughter—and with the hope? The following morning, 200 people filed into the room, looking as dazed as I had felt the day before. Some were crying. Most looked worried. Not one was laughing.

I began the talk I had prepared, called "Humor, Hugs, and Hope"—one I had given many times before, but never under such trying circumstances. To encourage laughter in a time of such overwhelming distress and uncertainty was the most help I could offer. It's what I do best. But under these conditions, would it help? Would it make a difference? I prayed that it would.

Throughout the talk, we laughed, we cried, we hugged, we talked about sources of hope—over and over again—for 90 minutes. I witnessed a miraculous change in the faces in front of me—and in my own heart. At the end of the talk, people gave me a standing ovation. Many also stopped by afterward to thank me, and we hugged again, seeking the reassurance of human touch in this time of tragedy.

But I knew that I was the one who should be thanking them. And that's just what I did—"I'm so glad I could be here!" I had been given an extraordinary opportunity that day. At a time when we all felt terribly helpless, I'd been given the chance to help, and I thanked God for it. I realized that, like those in my audience, I too had been healed by our laughter and tears—by our humor, hugs, and hope.

The Power of Shared Hope

For me, this event was the most gripping evidence of the extraordinary power of laughter, reassuring touch, and shared hope. But I have seen in a hundred small ways how important humor, hugs, and hope can be in our everyday lives. All three of these bring people together. They help us feel less alone in times of crisis, stress, and loss. Isn't it interesting how often we hear ripples of laughter at funerals when we recall funny stories about the person we loved? Isn't it striking how naturally we turn to one another for the comfort of hugs in times of loss?

Hope doesn't necessarily produce laughter, but laughter helps us feel hopeful. If we can still laugh, it's possible to go on. If we remind ourselves of our sources of hope, we can find reasons to continue in the midst of tragedy. If humor could help those 200 meeting participants carry on in the aftermath of 9/11, what could it *not* help us with?

So how can we get more of such miraculous benefits—and get more humor, hugs, and hope in our lives? I suggest focusing on the following four ways.

#1. Learn to Laugh at Yourself

If you can laugh at yourself, how much more humor will you have in your life? One topic alone—"my most embarrassing moments"—can evoke an abundance of funny stories. Here's just one of mine.

As you probably do, I get dozens of flyers every month announcing seminars designed to help me improve my business or personal life. One flyer really caught my eye. It advertised an April seminar titled "Getting Organized"— something people who know me would say I really need. (One of my favorite cartoons shows a desk foot-deep in papers and files, with the admonishment: "Those people who are so proud of having a neat desk will never know the joy of finding something they thought they had lost forever.")

I put the flyer into my April folder, thinking that I'd attend it if I had time when April rolled around. Sure enough, finding that flyer again in April, I realized I had the day free. I got excited at the prospect of attending the seminar. With this workshop, I would get my life organized and surprise everyone!

On the appointed date, I drove to the hotel, arrived on time, and scanned the hotel's list of conferences to find the room. I couldn't locate the listing, so I went to the front desk to ask where the "Getting Organized" seminar was being held. "There's no such meeting here," the young man informed me. "Isn't this the ____ hotel?" I retorted. "Yes, sir, it is." I plunged on, my flyer in hand, pointing to the relevant lines. "And isn't this April 22?" "Well yes, sir, it is." "So where is this meeting?" He didn't know. He only knew that no such group was holding a meeting at the hotel that day.

Angry, I called the toll-free number on my brochure to complain. How dare this group promise to help others get organized when they themselves were so disorganized that they couldn't even organize their own meeting effectively? The representative who answered listened to my frustration, apologized, then asked me the number of the course printed on the brochure. I gave it to her and fumed as I waited for her to return to the phone. A minute later, she was back. "Sir," she said, "I don't know how to tell you this, but that particular 'Getting Organized' session was April 22 of LAST year."

Can you imagine how this added humor to her day? Couldn't our own mistakes and foibles provide us with an endless (and constantly self-replenished) source of humor?

#2. Gather Other People's Stories

If you can get other people to share their embarrassing moments, you can also share in the fun of them. This is a great HP—"Humor Producer." Ask other people for their funny stories and embarrassing moments. We're rich repositories of humorous tales—you, me, family and friends, coworkers, and relative strangers. Often simply asking, "What funny things have happened in your job?" yields priceless anecdotes.

#3. Don't Lose the Funny Stories and Memories You Already Have

If you tried to estimate how often you had laughed at a certain funny incident or story during the past ten years, what would be your guess? If you averaged even one laugh a week, you'd have logged 520 "HMs"—humorous moments. Twice a week would double that number to more than 1,000. Yet, if I asked you right now to tell me a funny, true story—for a hundred-dollar bill—could you? No! More likely, you'd think a few moments, then admit: "I know that lots of funny things have happened, but I can't even think of one right now." I hear this all the time. We need a way to record these humorous moments so we don't lose them forever.

I keep a small 3" x 5" spiral notebook with me at all times. I keep this notebook in my shirt pocket, with a pen attached to it. My goal is to find at least three funny things a day—or three signs of hope—and record them on the spot so I can re-experience their benefits over and over again.

I record jokes, true stories, funny signs in stores or on the highway, remarks that I overhear—or mis-hear. Once at an annual church camp, I sat at a large table while two friends reconnected with each other, apparently after many years. The gray-haired man asked his friend, "What class are you taking at camp this week?" "Oh, I'm taking drums," she responded. "That's interesting—did you bring your own or does the camp supply them?" She smiled, "Oh, I brought my own—believe it or not, I still have some drums from the '60s."

With all the noise and my hearing challenges, I misheard one little word during this conversation. But it turned out to be a rather crucial word: I heard "drugs," not "drums." I'm no pharmacist, but I didn't think it would be a good idea to take drugs left over from the '60s! And then, to think that the church camp might supply them!

As I was calculating that her drugs would be 40 years old, I finally caught the word they had actually been saying—drums! We all howled when I explained my laughter to them. I think mistakes like this will just get worse (or better!) as we age. Listen to what you hear and mishear. It can be humor in disguise ("HID").

I bet you a million smackeroos that for every funny, touching incident we remember, we forget a hundred others. So get that small notebook, or write on a napkin, your shirt, your hand, or a wall — write it down and take a photo of it. Find some way not to *lose* it so you can relive these incidents and share them with others.

#4. Find More Hugs and Hope in Your Life

Hugs can bring humor, lightness, and laughter to many situations. To have more hugs in your life, the simplest ways is to ask for them—yet we often don't. Sometimes I give "hug coupons" out to members of my audiences. "Use these like a credit card," I tell them. "Show them to someone you trust; say 'Everyone is supposed to have at least 12 hugs a day for good health,' and ask them if they can spare a hug." One woman taped her hug coupon onto her refrigerator. She called me a

HUG COUPON
GOOD FOR ONE FREE HUG.
FREE HUG
REDEEMABLE FROM ANY CONSENTING HUMAN BEING.

"Show them to someone you trust; say 'Everyone is supposed to have at least 12 hugs a day for good health,'

month later to tell me this small action resulted in her teenage daughter wanting to hug her more in the past month than in the entire previous year. "My daughter just goes to the fridge, takes down the coupon, and says, 'I need to redeem this.' Somehow, the coupon made it possible for her to ask for a hug when she needs one, when she just couldn't before."

It's understandable that we sometimes hesitate to ask for a hug — we risk rejection. When my dad was dying, the doctor told me on the phone that if I wanted to say goodbye to my father, I'd better get there quick—I probably had only ten minutes. It took me 30 minutes to race to the hospital. When I got there, my dad lay on a cart in the emergency room, still breathing. I leaned over him, told him that I loved him, and gave him a hug. It was the first hug we'd shared in decades. I was afraid it would also be the last.

But my father is Swedish, and Swedes are known for their stubbornness. My father was so stubborn that he survived that day. A week later when I visited him at home, I thought I had a chance to change things between us. So toward the end of my visit, I said, "Dad, I was thinking—maybe we could hug when we say 'hello' and 'goodbye.' What do you think?" He looked at me with his beautiful blue eyes and said, "I think you're crazy!" Crestfallen, I put my jacket on. Apparently nothing would change.

But as I got to the doorway, there stood my dad. "Oh, well, if you're going to be all out-of-joint about it, all right, we can do that."

Those early hugs were awkward, so stiff and uncomfortable. But I persisted, and little by little, they became warmer, more comforting, more real. Then about two months later, I was rushing out of the house, late for an appointment. As I headed to my car, my father yelled from the doorway: "Hey! Hey! We forgot to . . . do that . . . thing . . ." He didn't know the word, but he knew that he missed it.

If a 76-year-old Swede can learn to hug, who can't? The gift that we receive when we ask for the comfort of a hug is worth the risk.

What Gives Us Hope?

Hugs and laughter, children, family and friends, a new day, a small step forward in achieving a goal, our religion or faith— all these can give us hope. What gives you hope? If you remind yourself of the sources of hope in your life, then you'll be able to use these to uplift yourself when you feel discouraged.

Did you know that every state in the United States except Hawaii has a city called Hope? And what do you think is the size of those cities — big or small? These are tiny towns. The "Hope map" reminds us to look for hope around us every day. Like these little cities, hope is there, though it's sometimes hard to find.

About the Author

Greg Risberg, CSP, MSW

G reg is a warm, funny motivational speaker whose presentations have been described as "hilariously informative." Greg has addressed everyone from nurses and teachers to bankers and farmers, traveling to 48 states, as well as Canada, Great Britain, and Australia. In his "humor with a message" programs, Greg offers useful ways to improve communication, handle stress, and increase humor and hope in people's lives.

The National Speakers Association has recognized Greg as a Certified Speaking Professional. Greg has a B. A. degree in Psychology and a Master's Degree in Social Work. He is the author of two books: *Touch: A Personal Workbook* and the soon-to-be-published *52 Ways To Fill Your Life with Humor, Happiness and Hope!*

Contact Information:

Greg Risberg, CSP, MSW, PFG*
Open Arms Seminars
295 E. Church St.
Elmhurst, IL 60126

Phone: 630-833-5066 • Fax: 630-833-5076
www.gregrisberg.com • E-mail: greg@gregrisberg.com
*Pretty Funny Guy

The Perfect World

by Scott Friedman, CSP

I can't tell you what I discovered about the concept of a Perfect World without telling you where it all started. So let the "perfect" journey begin.

The year was 1989. It was another beautiful Colorado summer morning like any other: 60 degrees, bright blue sky, a few cotton-like clouds. I was getting ready to leave my office to give the 300th speech of my career. (Of course the first 232 were for service clubs like Optimist, Rotary, Parents Without Partners, and Parents Without a Lot of Other Things, Too.) I had just started to make a few bucks in the speaking business, had recently bought a house, and felt pretty good about my future. I was living the good life; after all, I was President of the Colorado Chapter of the National Speakers Association. They don't elect just anyone you know. Or do they? Of course they don't.

The phone rang. It was a stranger, Nancy McGraw. She needed information. The President of the Colorado Speakers Association would surely have it. Did I know of any public seminar companies that were hiring? She was looking for part-time work as an on-site person for a public seminar company. They're the ones who handle registration on site, sell the products, and stand at the back of the room while the speaker is speaking, absorbing all of those wonderful ideas. Nancy had done a little work for Seminars International in the D.C. area before moving to Colorado. Did I know of anyone hiring?

"I don't, but why don't you come talk with me and see if you'd like to work for a professional speaker." Nancy came in the next day and hasn't left. Not that I wanted her to.

After one year, we found that "one thing" that Jack Palance talks about in *City Slickers*. That one thing that, when you find it, you know it—exactly what you've been looking for—the panacea! Nancy and I were talking about how to work better together. How can we be more efficient and effective in the office? How can we highlight our strengths, and outsource or minimize our weaknesses? Out of the discussion came that one thing we knew we had been looking for . . . the Perfect World concept. How do we create each other's "Perfect World?"

Wouldn't it be nice in our employer/employee relationship if we created a situation in which we both did more of what we loved, outsourced what we didn't like, and focused on living true to our values? What a concept! In fact, that would be each of our job descriptions: to create each other's Perfect World. Simple, yet profound.

My Perfect World

"Okay," Nancy asked, "What is it for you? What drives you? What do you value? What is your Perfect World?"

"It's anything that revolves around fun and freedom," I said. "Freedom to come and go as I please, freedom to create, and freedom to make a difference in this world in ways I'd like. If you help me do that, I'll be one happy camper."

So what does creating my Perfect World mean for Nancy? A lot.

Nancy takes care of everything in the office, and takes care of many things in the house and even the garage. (We work out of my house.) She does all the stuff that doesn't show but makes all the difference in world.

In addition to running the office, she covers for me when needed, reminds me of birthdays two weeks out, and never lets me leave the house wearing one black sock and one blue sock. (Nice to have your own fashion police right there on staff.) She takes me to and picks me up from the airport, does whatever it takes to get mailings out on time, and will run errands all over town at any time of the day or night. And to this day she is the only person who has successfully surprised me on my birthday. How clever, throwing me a surprise party at the airport in Denver for my fortieth birthday. As I came off the plane and saw my friends and family, I wondered where they all could be flying off to that day. Nothing like a good surprise as your mind slowly puts all the pieces together. I was truly floored by this great surprise—and tickled.

If you ask Nancy what she does for me, she loves to kid around by saying, "Everything except sex." Yes, if I'm in a bind—and I've been in quite a few binds—she'll do just about anything to create my Perfect World. Anything that is, except sex. After all, she *is* married and that "sex" stuff just doesn't have a place in the office.

Nancy's Perfect World

"Okay, Nancy, what is your Perfect World?" I asked.

"Get rid of anything to do with accounting and technology. Have more time for marketing and taking care of our clients. I'd also like to spend more time with my son, David (who at the time was 12), and with family around the country. I'd like to travel more, have more fun, and partake in the delightfully unexpected more often."

"Okay, done," I replied. "No more accounting and

technology. We'll order out. This will free you up to do more marketing and spend more time with clients. You can 'call in well' anytime you'd like if it gives you the opportunity to be with David and the family. We'll create an incentive plan and your reward will be free tickets to travel anywhere you'd like. And I'll do my best to keep things from getting mundane in the workplace.

"At the end of every month, we will grade ourselves on a scale of one to ten on how well we did at creating each other's Perfect World. If we aren't at a nine or ten, we'll figure out a way to raise the score the next month." And for the last 13 years, we've stayed in tune with each other's Perfect World.

The Perfect Birthday Surprise

Nancy's 50th birthday was a slam-dunk. Her son, David, her husband, Jack, and I etched the plot. David called about three weeks out and said, "Mom I feel terrible, but I can't come home for your birthday. I have three tests that week, and I can't make them all up. What if I came back two weeks later and then we'd have more time to spend together?" Nancy was disappointed, but she understood.

Fast forward to July 7, 2001, Nancy's 50th birthday. Being the loyal employee she is, Nancy is working a half day. About ten o'clock, the phone rings. It's my buddy Tim, but Nancy thinks it's a client. I answer and say, "You've made a decision, and you'd like me to speak on October 23rd in Orlando." I covered the phone. "Nancy, do me a quick favor, take my keys and run to the car and get my road calendar out of the trunk." (She'd done this before when I'd forgotten to bring in my calendar.) She goes to the car, opens the trunk, and sees David, who screams, "SURPRRIIIIIIISSEEE!"

After Nancy came to, she knew she was somewhere in the vicinity of her Perfect World. David had been happy to play along and was certainly glad he survived his time in the trunk. (It was only six hours — just kidding!)

The Perfect Raise

On to September 2001. Celebrating 13 wonderful years of working together, I wanted to give Nancy an "out-of-the-ordinary" raise and do it in a way she wouldn't soon forget. Anyone who can put up with me for 13 years deserves not only a medal, but something very special.

My "Keep the Fun Meter on a Ten" buddy, Gary, told me to lease Nancy a car. "Lease her a car that she wouldn't buy for herself, and she will appreciate it every day. (And the good news is, with the tax break, your gift goes twice as far.)"

What a brilliant idea. I mean a *perfect* idea. So I called Nancy's husband, Jack, to help with the latest scheme.

Here was the plan: Nancy's son, David, would fly out of Seattle one morning, and I'd pick him up at the airport on my way back from Colorado Springs where I had a speech. Nancy was scheduled to take my car in for servicing. That's where I'd drop David off. Clad in a mechanic's hat and glasses, David would drive up in a loaner from the service department, which would just happen to be her brand new car. In disguise, he'd say, "Ma'am, here is your loaner. Ahh, go ahead and just keep it. And you know what else? I'm coming with you!" He'd give her a big kiss and he'd drive her away. Seemed like the perfect plan.

It was the appointed day, a Tuesday in September. I awoke in a Colorado Springs hotel all excited about putting the plan into action. David would be at the airport in Seattle by now, ready to fly out. Nancy's husband, Jack, called me as I was about to go down to the meeting room. I already knew. I had been watching the Today Show as the second plane flew into the second World Trade Center tower.

Everything seemed surreal. They had closed all the airports around the country. David wouldn't be coming to Denver today. The planned surprise didn't seem like a big deal any more. Nothing did. A dark shadow had been cast over the world. With a lump in my throat, I went downstairs to fulfill my speaking engagement with the Rocky Mountain Telecommunications Association. I tried to offer hope.

After my program, I drove up to Denver from Colorado Springs. A friend and I picked up Nancy's new car. Instead of driving it to the dealership to drop off David, I drove it home and parked it in my neighbor's garage. Fortunately, my neighbor Marianne had an extra space and was willing to hide it.

Two mornings later, filled with sorrow and still in a daze, I knew it was time to take a break from our moping around. I remembered what I had told the Columbine school administrators at their year-end meeting soon after their tragedy: "Your job is not to stop mourning, but to stop *only* mourning. It's okay to take a break and celebrate what's good."

So I called Marianne and gave her the plan.

Here was the scene that morning: The phone rings in the office. Nancy answers. It's Marianne.

Nancy says to me, "Marianne thinks she left her coffeepot on. Could one of us run over and check? She said she gave you a garage door opener a few years back; do you still have it?"

I respond, "I think it's in the bottom drawer in the kitchen." Nancy finally finds the opener and heads over to check on the coffeepot. The first thing she sees when she opens the garage is a shiny new car. The way she tells the story, she's thinking, "Wow, Marianne got a new car. I wonder why she isn't driving it to work?" Then she sees a huge card on the car with NANCY in big letters written on it.

She opens the card and reads, "Happy 13 Years! Thanks for helping to create my Perfect World. I couldn't have done it without you."

Not sure if the car is really hers, but thinking it may be, she comes back to the house for an explanation with her mouth open, muttering, "Oh my gosh." More than once, I confirm the good news and ask if she turned off the coffeepot. In the midst of a very tough stretch, we take time to celebrate.

(One important note: I was in a fortunate circumstance to be able to afford a car for Nancy. You don't have to be that elaborate. A special card, a dinner at a wonderful restaurant, a certificate to get someone's windows cleaned—any extra and carefully thought-through gesture will have the same joyful effect.)

Creating Others' Perfect Worlds

What if we lived our life with each other's "Perfect World" in mind? What if we spent more time asking questions and paying attention to the Perfect World of our co-workers, spouses, family, and friends? What if we made choices in life based on those Perfect Worlds? Would you sell more? Would you laugh more? Would you love more? Would the quality of your relationships improve? Would the quality of your life improve?

So how do you best go about creating another person's Perfect World? You start by looking at the world through their eyes. It's not always easy if you only have eyes for "I." Get past your self-absorbed self. Pay more attention.

Start by asking questions. Ask the customers themselves: "If we could have done one thing better in working with you, what would it have been?" Find out and then deliver. Ask: How can I create a better experience for my customers? What can I do to truly connect with them? How can I move from being ordinary to extra-ordinary?

Do you want to keep good customers? Want to keep good friends? Want to keep good employees? Find out what drives them. Find out what constitutes their Perfect World.

According to the United States Department of Labor, 87% of employees leave their jobs because they are unhappy with their managers. Do you think those managers are tuned in to employee needs and values?

The University of California at Irvine School of Psychology and Human Behavior conducted a survey to determine motivating factors for employees. Would it surprise you that money ranked near the bottom? Appreciation, flexibility, challenging work, and good communication were the top four.

The most effective company incentive programs I've seen are the ones customized to meet the desires of each employee.

Ralph Waldo Emerson said, "One of the most beautiful compensations of this life is that no one can sincerely try to help another without helping himself." It's a wonderful way to live.

So, you may be asking, "What does this have to do with a book on humor?" Good question. Glad you asked. You see, humor doesn't always have to be about silliness and laughter. Humor evolves naturally from an atmosphere in which we have created delight. Take an environment free of sorrow, pain, and resentment, then enhance it with delight, and we have created a space for humor.

By living the "Perfect World" philosophy, we provide an opportunity for joy, spontaneity, curiosity, silliness, and laughter to flourish. And that's humor at its very best. In fact, that's . . . perfect!

About the Author

Scott Friedman, CSP

Scott teaches audiences to open their minds through laughter, while sharing "how to" techniques and practical ideas about humor, sales, and mastering change. He currently serves on the boards of directors for the National Speakers Association and Camp To Belong, a non-profit organization dedicated to reuniting siblings in foster care.

Scott has written *Using Humor for a Change, 101 Clever Ideas to 'Lighten Up' the Workload*, and *Punchlines, Pitfalls and Powerful Programs -10 Surefire Ways of Adding Humor to Your Presentations.*

Contact Information:

Scott Friedman, CSP
Scott Friedman & Associates
1563 S. Trenton Ct.
Denver, CO 80231-2617

Phone: 800-657-0019
www.FunnyScott.com
E-mail: Scott@FunnyScott.com

Rowing the Same Lifeboat
Humor and Friendship

by Kathleen Keller Passanisi, PT, CSP

"Among those whom I like or admire, I can find no common denominator.
But among those whom I love, I can; all of them make me laugh." — W.H. Auden

It was a typical day in my office. I was putting together a presentation while M.J. Ruff, my "right-arm, left-brain" friend and office administrator, was methodically working her way through the endless details of running my business. I paid little attention when the phone rang and she answered it with her energetic "Kathleen Passanisi's New Perspectives. This is M.J."

Normally there would be a pause as she listened, followed by her upbeat and polished response to whatever had been said. This time there was dead silence. I glanced over to see her ashen and frozen in place. The words she seemed to be searching for finally came out as, "Would you repeat that, please?" The voice on the other end of the phone repeated the message. "Mrs. Ruff, this is Bea calling from the nursing home. I hate having to tell you this, but we lost your father."

When M.J. looked at me and told me her dad was gone, I could imagine what she was feeling. My own father lives in a long-term care facility, and I dread the day when that call comes for me. She collected herself and asked when her father's passing occurred. The caller hesitated, then realizing the confusion, replied, "Oh no, ma'am; he's not dead. We just can't find him!"

Lewis had disappeared.

M.J. hung up, looking bewildered. In the space of a few short few moments, her emotions had roller-coastered from shock to loss to relief to concern. But as she related the story to me, something amazing happened. We burst out laughing in great guffaws, coupled with copious, cleansing tears. It was that marvelous kind of belly laughter that makes you feel as though you've run a marathon. When the adrenaline gets used up, you're spent.

Lewis was found later that day at a local MiniMart. Although it was frightening to have a loved one with Alzheimer's disease missing, it was better than having him dead.

Emotional Balance

Why were we laughing over something so heart-wrenching? If others had been around, they might have judged us to be uncaring or incredibly insensitive. And what had happened to rebalance M.J.'s emotions so quickly?

I thought back over the years of our friendship that began as college freshmen. In those days, we laughed about picky professors, unreasonable curfews, and "mystery meat" meals. These days, we call ourselves poster women for the "sandwich generation." Dealing with dwindling savings, college tuition, weddings, and funerals, we're too busy for a mid-life crisis. In spite of life's rapids and whirlpools, we don't need therapy because we laugh together all the time. We're co-captains of the same lifeboat!

Powerful Combination

Why is the combination of laughter, humor, and friendship so powerful?

Laughter has long been referred to as "good medicine." Scientists have found that a good belly laugh can relax muscle tension, exercise the heart and lungs, improve circulation, and increase oxygen flow throughout the body. Laughter plays a role in strengthening the immune system. It also helps prevent stress hormones that can have a wide range of adverse effects, some life-threatening.

Humor is usually the precursor to laughter. Because humor is based on an individual's unique way of perceiving things, a sense of humor can vary greatly from person to person. What causes one to fume may prompt another to crack a joke. One passenger may view lost luggage as a disaster, and set off a full-blown stress response. Another may find the situation funny, and laugh heartily about it. In doing so, he or she maintains a neutral, or positive, emotional state.

When you add the element of friendship to laughter and humor, the results are often dramatic. Why? Because when you're alone during times of stress, you're more likely to "awfulize," or see the worst. You may blow the problem way out of proportion. But if you see your situation through the eyes of a friend who has walked in your Nikes—one who's been able to see the humor in it with the passage of time—you'll rebound faster. You may even avoid the unpleasant aftermath altogether.

This is why M.J. recovered so quickly that day in the office. Had she been by herself or with someone who didn't understand the difficulties of dealing with aging parents, she might have sat down and bawled. Because she had a friend nearby, she was able to cope by laughing instead. That's the power of Humor + Laughter + Friendship. When it comes to well-being, it's the equivalent of 1 + 1 + 1 = 100!

It Happens to Everyone

Imagine the following situation. You are working away in your office cubicle and decide to take a bathroom break. In the washroom, you run into your buddy Angelo who asks, "What's shakin', friend?" You tell him you're swamped with work because your boss, Old Man Grimsley, doesn't know the first thing about managing the workload. You commiserate for a moment until you hear a flushing sound. The conversation stops. Your heart stops. And who steps out of the stall? You guessed it—Old Man Grimsley. He says nothing as he washes his hands. You mumble something imbecilic. He glares and walks out. Your job and financial security flash before your eyes. You're wondering if you could be any dumber. Cringing, Angelo says "Ouch" and leaves you alone. The panic, racing heart, dry mouth, rapid breathing, and muscle tension show up as by-products of a big-time stress response that plague you for the rest of the afternoon.

After work, you decide to fortify yourself with a quick drink before heading home and confessing your stupidity to your pregnant wife. At the local hangout, you join a group of co-workers and find Angelo regaling them with the story of your grand goof. What happens? Everyone laughs. The next thing you know, they're all sharing similar stories, each one worse than the other. You feel better because they've made gaffes that were equally awful. They are laughing "with" you—not "at" you. Laughing at their stories helps you shorten the time it takes to shift your perspective from "tragic" to "comic." Your co-workers and friends are credible when they reassure you it's not the end of the world; life will go on. If others who have never been in this situation make light of your problem, you'll probably feel misunderstood or resentful at their insensitivity in minimizing your trouble.

Every stage of life has its challenges. Whether we laugh or cry about them depends on our perception of the situation. What often seems like tragedy in the beginning evolves into comedy over time.

When you can shorten the time it takes to go from tragedy to comedy, you'll have mastered one of the most effective ways to manage stress!

Laugh Today

Now, please don't misunderstand; *some* things in life will never be funny, no matter how much time goes by. Fortunately, it's not *most* things. How do you distinguish between what will be funny and what won't? I encourage my audiences to remember this: "If it's going to be funny tomorrow, you might as well laugh today!"

The emotional element of pain is frequently great grist for humor. Analyze any situation comedy and you'll discover that the humor is usually based on the character's frustrations, mistakes, embarrassments, disappointments, plans gone awry, and the like. If you see your life as a situation comedy, you'll discover an endless source of funny material.

Recognize These Scenarios?

Look back on your life and you'll probably find you've befriended people whose trials and tribulations have paralleled your own in some ways.

Remember grade school and your best friend, Leon? Both of you had that awful math teacher, referred to as Mizzzz Felcher—the one with the moustache. You and Leon disliked school, hated math, and constantly joked about giving Fuzz-Face Felcher a razor for Christmas. United against a common enemy, you laughed yourselves silly.

Move on to high school. What bonded you to your laughing pals? If you couldn't get a date, didn't you find things to laugh about with the other "dateless wonders?" If you were a crummy athlete, didn't you and your uncoordinated pals crack each other up making armpit noises and belching in front of the cheerleaders?

In college, friends who had already experienced being dumped helped ease your despair when yet another romance went down the tubes. Brokenhearted, you tearfully shared your latest tragedy with them. They listened, then proceeded to one-up you with their own soap opera stories. Because time had passed since their traumas, they had already moved from misery through the stage of fantasizing ingenious methods of revenge to the crystal clarity of hindsight. Their hilarious stories taught you valuable lessons. In no time, tears of loss and rejection changed to tears of laughter. That's when the healing began. What started off as the narrow "Poor me. No one will ever love me!" broadened to "Good grief! What did I ever see in that toad? I deserve better—someone with taste."

In the Same Boat

If you follow this course of thinking, it's easy to see that one finds comfort and relief with others who are, or have been, in the same boat. New moms who get very little sleep gravitate to each other for laughter and support. Guys with lousy golf games much prefer the company of other duffers to serious players. Facing possible layoffs, coworkers will often share gallows humor as a way to cope with their fears. Even the elderly will entertain their peers with a story about retrieving a $750 hearing aid from the toilet; the episode involving the nasty word their three-year-old grandchild blurted out in church has the bingo group in stitches.

I once overheard my mother talking with her longtime friend. In a highly serious tone Mom said, "You know, Margaret, these days I spend a lot of time pondering the hereafter." Both being in their eighties, Margaret sighed and nodded with understanding. A wry smile spread across Mom's face as she quickly added, "I walk into a room and think, now what in the hell did I come in *here after*?" Both of them burst out laughing, grabbed their walkers, and headed for separate restrooms. (Note: the combination of a full bladder and belly laughter can produce the only known negative side effect of humor—temporary incontinence.)

I know my mother must have heard that joke somewhere and had been saving it for just the right moment. She and Margaret were old friends. They had been through miscarriages, kid-raising, multiple surgeries, empty nests, and debilitating arthritis. Together, they could find humor in just about anything.

What Steals Laughter?

We all want a high quality of life, and *that* involves good health and happiness. Laughter and humor associated with friendship contribute immeasurably—and they're free! So, what keeps us from capitalizing on them? Too often, it's culprits such as "busyness" and "isolation."

Is your day a recurring blur of activity? See if this sounds familiar: You crawl out of bed before dawn. While packing lunches and signing field trip permission slips, you call your mother and beg her to sit with little Brianna who can't go to nursery school because of a goopy nose. Stuck in rush-hour gridlock, you notice your SUV is running on fumes. That means you'll be late again for a meeting with your grouchiest client. Lunch consists of stale pretzels from the vending machine, eaten while trying to reduce the number of your e-mails to less than three figures. You cancel yet another dental appointment so that you can drive Trevor to "select team" soccer. Arriving home after dark, you throw something from a box into the microwave. Dinner disintegrates while you tackle paying the bills. Although you doze off watching Jay Leno, you're wide-awake two hours later, wondering why you can't sleep when you're totally exhausted!

Life as a single person is no less hectic. You run with the dog before sun-up. An hour later, you're crammed into the subway with really strange strangers. You speed-walk the remaining five blocks to the office in the pouring rain. Along the way, you drop off your dry cleaning, use the ATM, and grab a four-dollar latte. Although you take no breaks and work two extra hours, you can't seem to catch up. Running late, you spend $30 on a taxi to get to your MBA class. Midnight finds you alone on your couch in your $1800-a-month studio apartment, drinking a low-carb beer and eating a quart of Ben and Jerry's. The message on your machine is from your mother, letting you know that your cousin (the ugly one) is engaged to a doctor.

Negative Effects of Loneliness

Feel like you're all alone? Rest assured, plenty of others are sharing this boat with you. In spite of the growing world population, an increasing number of people suffer the negative effects of loneliness—from depression to reduced longevity.

Look at the trends. In 1950, one out of ten people lived alone. In 2000, it was one in four. We marry later, if at all. Divorce is more prevalent. We bear fewer children. We're more likely to move away from family and friends. We're so pressed for time that we have little left for activities involving quality face-time with others. And, although communication technology is supposed to help us connect with others, researchers tell us that e-mail and chat rooms may actually add to our sense of isolation.

Staying Afloat

Face it. Stress is a part of life that's not going away. If you don't learn to deal with it, it can pull you down. Don't let that happen. The next time the seas of life get choppy, remember the sentiment expressed by W.H. Auden; those friends you love are usually those who help you to laugh. Reach out for them and let the laughter buoy you. Where are they when you need help? They're rowing the lifeboat!

Five Important Steps

To benefit from the combination of humor, laughter, and friendship in your life, make a point of doing these five things:

1. Take a serious look at how you spend your time.

2. Analyze your activities to see if they contribute to your health and happiness.

3. Think about the people you spend time with. Do they bring you down? Is it time to replace them with more upbeat people?

4. Make a list of friends you easily laugh with.

5. Schedule face-time with these friends no less than once a week. Get together for the sole purpose of laughing together. Make it a priority.

Dedicated to all my friends with whom I laugh during turbulent times.

You know who you are.

About the Author

Kathleen Keller Passanisi, PT,CSP

Recipient of the 2003 Lifetime Achievement Award from the Association for Applied and Therapeutic Humor, Kathleen has helped nearly a gazillian people shift their perspectives and find humor in everyday life. Whether with rocket scientists or cancer patients, cardiologists or married couples, Passansi's programs have packed corporate meeting rooms, health care facilities, and convention centers.

A licensed health care professional, Kathleen is also the self-proclaimed poster woman of the *Sandwich Generation*. In a world plagued by stress, she shares her tools for coping with the unexpected, the unavoidable, and even the unbearable circumstances of life.

Contact Information:

Kathleen Passanisi, PT, CSP
New Perspectives
Lake Saint Louis, MO

Phone: 636-561-2516
Fax: 636-561-2520
www.kathleenpassanisi.com
kathleen@kathleenpassanisi.com

Making a Difference
Humor That Takes You Beyond Yourself

by Craig Zablocki

When I was 20 years old, I took time off from college to travel. Sitting on a beach in Fiji, I opened M. Scott Peck's book *The Road Less Traveled*. The first line says, "Life is difficult." (I found that out soon enough. A few years later, my beloved older sister was killed while running on Maui. Her murderer was never found. My family and I will never be the same. This is a fact in my life. Yet I still laugh. I need to.)

A few weeks into my trip to Fiji, I jumped aboard a local fishing boat for a ride to one of the outer islands. I stayed in a village whose inhabitants survive with much less than I was used to in America—specifically, no electricity, no running water, no hot showers. They lived off the land and traded tapa cloth they made from indigenous trees for staples such as sugar and rice.

One night at dinner, I was sitting on the ground eating with my fingers, mosquitoes humming around my head. I swatted them wildly, trying to eat. I must have looked ridiculous because one elderly woman started laughing and saying something in Fijian. Everyone began to hoot and holler. Not even knowing what was funny, I started laughing with them. At that moment, I felt accepted and part of the village.

That evening after dinner, faint sounds of drumming, singing, and laughter piqued my curiosity. I walked in the dark for several minutes and stumbled on a tiny hut where dozens of children, ages two to 18, were sitting around a blazing fire and singing with abandon. The scene mesmerized me. The children looked so joyful, so filled with happiness, so utterly living in the moment. I stood motionless, transfixed.

A few days later, I attended a three-day funeral for one of the older men who'd passed away. The first day, everyone grieved together, crying over their loss. The second and third days, they spent celebrating the man's life—sharing stories, dancing, singing, and feasting in honor of their friend.

These people lived genuinely joyful lives. They told me that suicide, depression, and violence did not exist in their village. Amazing.

Miracles of That Summer

Six months after my sister's death, I found myself depressed, sad, and angry. I felt helpless and hopeless; the emotional pain seemed intolerable. I desperately needed some perspective on the world, so I quit my full-time job as a restaurant manager and took a job as a cook at a wilderness camp for kids. As I look back on that summer, I remember how the miracles then set me on the path to healing.

The healing environment of nature surrounded me, and the simple act of cooking for kids genuinely delighted me. On top of that, the kids themselves were pure pleasure.

One day, Sam, one of my favorite campers, snuck into the kitchen with a puppet he'd made. "Craig, this is Wally my puppet," he said to me. He then spoke in a strange voice with great animation as if he were the puppet. With every word, Sam's mouth opened wider, not even attempting to be a ventriloquist. The more animated the puppet became, the more animated Sam became. His enjoyment of performing started me laughing. Sam joined in, both of us laughing so hard that tears rolled down our cheeks.

When I returned to my cabin, I sat on my bed and realized that I felt *different*; very different from the day I'd received word of my sister's murder. I wondered what had accounted for the shift. Then the revelation hit. A boy with a puppet had softened my heart and allowed me, for the first time in months, to surrender to laughter. Laughter brought me to a place from which I'd been away for a long time. It felt good to be back.

Healing Power of Humor

With that epiphany, my life took a turn. I decided to devote my time to speaking about the healing power of humor. I started giving speeches across the country, sharing how humor can help with grieving and overcoming tragedy.

Years after that summer camp, I spoke to families of slain police officers in Washington D.C. Throughout my speech, I laughed and cried, as did many in the audience. After one speech, a woman approached with tears in her eyes and explained that her husband had been killed nine months earlier. She introduced me to her father-in-law, who hadn't smiled since the death of his son, but to her amazement laughed out loud during my talk. Excited, she gave me a hug and said, "You brought life back to my father-in-law."

Being able to laugh is critical to healing. Psychologists say that when someone's sense of humor comes back, they're on the road to recovery. My 57-year-old friend Harvey was a man with a loving family, a great sense of humor, and a passion for photography. One day, while crossing a road to take pictures, he was hit by a truck and died instantly. A few days later, family and friends gathered in his living room to mourn his passing.

The mood of the group had been somber for quite some time. Then Harvey's son, Rich, appeared at the top of the stairs after picking out a burial suit for his dad. Harvey collected hats and Rich announced that he'd found the perfect hat for his father to wear. We looked at him with curiosity. From behind his back, Rich brought out a baseball hat that said, "Shit happens." There was a pause, a *lonnnggg* pause, then everyone burst into laughter. It lasted for at least five minutes. We felt Harvey was laughing with us.

We can't control much of what life throws at us. But when we laugh, we make a choice. We can't control what happens— the setbacks, the heartbreak—but we can choose how to respond. Victim advocates, social workers, police officers, and firefighters have high rates of burnout, depression, alcoholism, and broken families. Their exposure to tragedy and death is a daily reality. How do they survive their jobs? The ones who survive use humor every day to balance the difficulties of their everyday work.

Through the Worst of Times

Humor is a universal coping method that can get you through the worst of times. Remember the television show *M*A*S*H* — one of the most popular sit-coms of all time. It depicted a group of doctors and nurses in the midst of a senseless war, surrounded by bloodshed and death, but coping—and surviving—with humor.

The movie *Life is Beautiful* follows a little boy and his father who were living in a concentration camp during World War II. The father refocuses the grim realities of war into a game, a game the boy could play. The movie illustrates how one man's imagination and immense sense of humor saved his family.

Acceptance is the key. As the Serenity Prayer says, "God grant me the serenity to accept the things I cannot change, the courage to change the things I can, and the wisdom to know the difference."

In our society, anger is prevalent. However, beneath anger there's always hurt, sadness, and fear. What if we were more emotionally honest? What if we could express sadness and joy instead of rage? What would happen if we took ourselves *lightly*?

no Volunteers

In a talk to a group of 650 school superintendents, I started my speech with a request. I said, "I need a volunteer to help me with an activity. It will be fun, you'll learn something new, and you'll be supported. Who would like to help me?" To my amazement, no one volunteered.

With much curiosity, I stepped into the audience and

asked, "Why do you think no one put his hand up right now?" I waited for a response. Everyone in the audience was stone-faced, the air thick with peer pressure.

Finally, I asked, "If I were to walk into a kindergarten class in your district and ask the same question, how many hands do you think would go up in the air?" The response, from those who spoke up, was, "All of them."

I agreed and asked, "How about those in your fifth-grade class?" The response from someone in the crowd was, "More than half."

That's what I've experienced as well. Younger kids are more likely to volunteer, and love doing so. With older kids, self-consciousness has kicked in and fewer put up their hands.

Then I posed these questions to the group of superintendents: When was the last time you asked a teenager for advice? When was the last time you were with a group of kids and you laughed so hard, pieces of lunch flew out of your mouth? That is, when was the last time you were willing to make yourself vulnerable and to risk appearing foolish? Why, as we get older, is this so hard to do?

Appearances Don't Matter

Many of us have experienced that crying—either from joy or sadness—is cathartic. Holding back our tears can lead to anger, anxiousness, and depression. That's more reason to laugh so hard that we cry (or cry so hard that we laugh). When we hold back, we trade appearances for the opportunity to heal.

I spoke at Columbine High School a few months after the shooting tragedy experienced there in 1999. I will never forget the strength of Columbine's principal, Frank DeAngelis. It wasn't what he *said* that day or any day since. It was how he so openly displayed his feelings to his students.

On several occasions, he laughed and cried in front of his school and, in doing so, he gave permission to students, teachers, and support staff to be emotional, to be human, to laugh when something struck them as funny, to dissolve in tears when sadness was overwhelming. To do otherwise is to deny something essentially human in all of us.

One day, long ago when I was a teacher, I noticed two guys in the hall provoking one another, fists clenched, ready to fight. Cheering teenagers surrounded them. I made my way to the middle of the pack, approached one young man and shouted, "Kevin, your zipper is down." As he looked down at his fly, his hands began to relax. He realized I was teasing him. He looked up with a grin and his opponent started laughing. With humor and these boys' willingness to laugh at themselves, this potentially violent situation was defused.

My son, Charles was three years old when, one day after swimming, we found ourselves in the dressing room of the athletic club surrounded by an entire team of half-dressed rugby players. These dudes were big and they were tough. The smell of Brut hung in the air.

Out of the blue, Charles breaks into the "Alphabet Song," the one that goes "A, B, C, D," and so on. Standing next to him was one of the tougher guys; King Kong to be exact. He looks down at Charles, hesitates for a moment, and then joins this little boy, singing with total commitment. Before long, we all are belting out our ABCs, together. Picture this: 20 grown men, half-dressed, led in song by a three-year-old. Who took themselves seriously in this locker room?

Tips for Tough Times

The best tips for tough times are to let go, be childlike, innocent, and vulnerable. Be open to the different emotions you might have and don't worry if they're appropriate or not. Here are my suggestions for making it through tough times:

- **Take yourself lightly:** Let go of the idea that you are the center of the universe, all important. Take what's in your heart and soul seriously, but abandon the need to keep up an image, whether it's acting tough, cool, intelligent, strong, or invulnerable to feelings. Be real, without pretense, as if you were four years old again. Go to a playground and watch the children interact. There's no posturing among young kids; they're out to have a good time.

- **Laugh:** Laughter can annihilate the ego, and believe me, that's just what the ego needs. It's impossible to laugh and, at the same time, feel heavy-hearted. Other emotions get deep-sixed for the duration of the laugh, maybe longer, so let laughter rule as much as you can every day.

As adults, we tend to replay the past and feel sad or contemplate the future with trepidation. If nothing else, laughter rivets us to the here and now. For a few moments, we may be able to forget ourselves. Michael Prichard, a comedian, once said, "Laughter is like changing a diaper—it doesn't get rid of the problem; it just makes things more bearable for a while." So, surround yourself with people and things that tickle your funny bone.

- **Honor your emotions:** If you feel the urge to cry, do it. If you feel the urge to laugh, do it. Young children feel a myriad of emotions each day. They feel them, they express them, and they allow the feelings to pass. Because depression comes from the repression of emotions, seek out supportive people who allow you to fully express your emotions without judgment. And don't judge your emotions either; whatever you feel is exactly right.

- **Laugh with others (versus at others):** Positive humor—humor that is not at anyone's expense—combines love and joy. Negative humor can hurt. You can find so many ironies, paradoxes, and things worth a laugh—from the simple to the absurd. Allow yourself to be delighted by the spontaneous laughter of children. Find the opportunities for laughter that surround you, then give in to them. Life is truly funny.

- **Say "I don't know":** Children admit when they don't know and don't feel shame about not knowing. Often, adults are reluctant to admit they don't know and are afraid to be curious. Because of this, learning comes to a screeching halt.

We need to grow throughout our lives, despite the fact there's so much we'll never understand no matter how much we watch CNN. There's so much we don't know, so much we don't even *know* that we don't know. So, fess up. It's freeing.

Two Choices

What choices do we have when confronted with the inevitable losses and confrontations life brings? After all, Scott Peck was right. Life *is* difficult. We can't laugh away terrorism, disease, famine, or any of our tragedies. But as my father said, days after my sister's death, we have two choices: We can become bitter, cynical, and resigned, or, through this experience, we can choose to make a difference.

The choice is ours. Humor can help. It may not be able to undo what has happened but it can help us accept and move on from places we thought we never could.

After my sister's death, I thought I would never feel joy again. Today, my experience of helping others through humor has brought immeasurable joy and meaning to my life. Maybe it can for you, too.

Tips for Tough Times

Take yourself lightly

Laugh

Honor your emotions

Laugh with others (versus at others)

Say "I don't know"

About the Author

Craig Zablocki

A nationally known speaker and consultant, Craig has spoken to over 600,000 people internationally and in all 50 states. He has shared the platform with President George W. Bush, Tom Peters, and Al Gore. Craig presents to Fortune 500 companies, legislators, public service and healthcare professionals, college campuses, non-profit service organizations, and victim rights groups. He was the first outside speaker to address the student body of Columbine High School after its tragedy.

Craig's unscripted style has been compared to a hybrid of Robin Williams and Wayne Dyer. One participant wrote, "We should harness his energy - it could power a small city. His passion and commitment to making a difference is contagious!"

Contact Information:

Craig Zablocki
634 Marion St.
Denver, CO 80218

Phone: 303.830.7996 • Fax: 303.830.0194
www.PositivelyHumor.com • craig@PositivelyHumor.com

Preparation H For The Soul

by Michael Rayburn

There I was, 13 years old, locked in my basement bedroom. My dad, hearing strange, muffled sounds from inside began knocking on my door demanding, "Son, what's going on in there?" Knowing it was something I shouldn't be doing, I didn't answer. He got angry. "Michael, you open this door right now!" He could hear me fumbling around, panicking. "Uh, just a minute," I managed. Too late. The door flew open and there I was, caught, with the contraband in my hand. Yep, just what you're thinking—a Richard Pryor album. Waaaay off limits to a 13-year old back then. I had been listening with the volume low when Dad knocked.

And with that, ladies and gentlemen, my dreams of making people laugh went into the closet—where they would stay for a long time.

I tell you this now, as a simple matter of practicality as much as motivation: If you have a dream, a grand dream, of doing something you love, something you feel called to do, whatever it is, just get on with it. Put this book down and start right now. It will bug you until you do. Dreams are like hemorrhoids—they keep itching at you, they never go away, and they always find their way to the surface, no matter what. (I guess now we're all glad this chapter isn't illustrated) Ahhh . . . but when you finally embrace the dream it's like . . . Preparation H for the Soul! (Hmmm, I can feel a big ol' book series coming on.)

While I always knew I wanted to be a guitar player, the dream of doing comedy bugged me for more than 20 years before I finally and fully trusted it. All the while, though, it slowly, doggedly kept at me.

In junior high school, with an influence no less than that of a bible on a disciple, my friend, Dan Rosen, loaned me an Arlo Guthrie album called "Alice's Restaurant." For those unfamiliar with this song, it is a magnificently bizarre story spun into a Vietnam protest song which is 18 minutes, 20 seconds long. (Ironically, this is the exact amount of time mysteriously erased from Nixon's Whitehouse tapes. Coincidence? I think not.) Anyway, the song is outrageous, it is hilarious, and I couldn't get enough of it! Every day when I got home from school, I would head straight for the record player with that album, my mom ordering (or pleading), "Only TWO TIMES!" Had she known the alternative was Richard Pryor maybe she wouldn't have been so hard on Arlo. I'd have listened to it all afternoon. I have it memorized to this day. And though I couldn't have known it at the time, it gave me the basic formula I now use in every program I do: Use guitar and comedy to render a message. You see, laughter is wonderfully disarming; it puts people at ease and makes them much more receptive to what you have to say.

Scratching the Itch

In my college music program, I started off as a voice major but somehow the Italian aria and I never quite got along. They have something called master classes where you stand in a sterile little room and sing opera for the other voice majors and teachers, and they critique your voice and offer suggestions. It's a thoroughly unnerving experience. The ultimate goal in that environment is to sing like Pavarotti. When I finished my first song in Italian, no one said anything. Silent as a tomb. I began to shrink inside. Finally someone spoke up. "He sounds like Neil Young." She might as well have said Tiny Tim. It's like telling an aspiring Shakespearian actor, "Wow, you're like... Tony Danza." The opera instructor wrote in my evaluation, "You sing Italian country western very well." Not exactly a compliment.

You see, when you're not on the right path toward your dream, when you're not "following your bliss" as Joseph Campbell said, sooner or later the world will let you know. So, I became a guitar major and found my musical niche. Not that I intended to be a classical guitarist for a living; I just wanted to thoroughly learn the instrument and it just felt right.

In college, I also rediscovered folk music, a good portion of which now annoys me. Don't get me wrong, I love getting together with a group of songwriters playing songs for each other in a circle, but I guess I have heard one too many troubadours who endlessly bemoan and re-hash every bad experience, every guy or girl who ever dumped them, in dark, brooding songs that drone on and on. I call these songs "wrist-slashers" because, by the end, you just want to die. Of course, I never did die because they'd have only written a song about it—let them get their own material. Who was it who said, "If I had a hammer . . . there'd be no more folk singers?"

Anyway, even though I'd written one or two myself, by the time the circle got around to me and we'd heard five wrist-slashers in a row, I just couldn't do it. So I wrote a song called "You Done Me Wrong . . . (But At Least You Done Me)" for just those occasions. Crass? Sure. But profoundly necessary. And aha! I was beginning to use music and comedy—scratching the itch, so to speak.

I paid my way through college by playing clubs. Friends, there is no way to play 90-dollar, four-hour bar gigs for drunk people night after night without developing either a sense of humor or a drinking problem. Luckily I chose the former. I started having fun with the strange requests they would yell out under the "alcafluence of incahol." Though it was a slow evolution, more and more I was being booked for the funny stuff. Scratch, scratch.

There were two more pieces missing from the puzzle. The first was that while now my show was based largely on comedic songs and impressions like "Bob Marley sings Garth Brooks," I never actually called myself a comedian. I see now that I was giving myself an excuse in case I wasn't funny. Unfortunately, it was also a nice little buffer between me and . . . success. How often is it that we kinda, sorta, maybe do something hoping to get the success without risking the failure? Sooner or later you have to step up, lay it on the line.

And that I did. I convinced Zanie's comedy club in Nashville to give me a 10-minute set. In the first 15 seconds, my worst fear—a heckler—was realized. I opened with a short guitar piece and some guy in the first row yelled, "Freebird!" I thought, "How original, dude," but kept playing. Again, even louder he yelled, "I wanna hear Freebird!" and both the audience and I knew I had to respond. Without thinking, I kept playing with one hand and with the other lifted my middle finger replying, "There's your free-bird." The crowd howled!

Now, I wouldn't have done that anywhere else, but in that environment, it was just the right thing. And at that very moment after 15 years of performing, I became a comedian. I have never looked back.

Squeezing the Tube

There's an old phrase I have always found to be true: When the student is ready the teacher will appear. And thus did Jana Stanfield, a wonderful speaker and hit songwriter who uses her music as well as her words to deliver her message, appear at my comedy club shows. From Jana I learned so much more about incorporating my message into my programs. Also, she showed me a whole new marketplace—corporations and associations—for whom the message was often as important as the entertainment value. For me, entertaining and empowering people is so much better than selling beer for a comedy club. The final piece was in place. The guitar, the comedy, the message, and an audience ripe for all three. I can look back now and see how all these events lined up to bring me to this place, a place where I know I'm supposed to be. And, ahh . . . no more itching.

Soothing Relief

I truly have the greatest job in the world. I get to sit around and ask questions. Every one of us spends our lives asking questions of ourselves. Unfortunately, most of them are wonderfully empowering like, "Uh, how long 'til five o'clock?" "What's on TV tonight?" "Which chick is the Bachelor gonna pick?" You want a simple way to change your life? Ask better questions. Or funnier questions. Instead of, "Which girl is the Bachelor gonna pick?" how about, "What if 12 of the girls he has to choose from are female impersonators?" Now that show I would watch. (Announcer's voice: "And the Bachelor chooses . . . Frank!") And while we're on the subject, the Bachelor is always this young, good-looking, rich guy and I'm wondering—does this guy need a TV show to get a date? I mean, if they really want to help someone, how about poor little Erwin down at Moto-Foto with the acne problem?

The difference between comedians and normal people is that we have to be observant in order to update our material, to improve our shows, to, uh . . . eat. We have to notice what's going on and ask, "What's funny about this? What's missing here?" It just makes life more interesting to think that way. For example, at the country store near my home, I saw a guy with a serious frown holding a can of Raid in one hand and a six-pack of Budweiser in the other. I asked him, "You gonna get drunk and kill some bugs?" We laughed and the day was better. Most importantly, it's usually better not to think too hard about a response. Just open your mouth and let it come out (editing for appropriateness, of course).

I believe all comedy—all real creativity in fact—comes from beyond ourselves. The greatest creative minds of all time—from Mozart to Neil Simon—credit an outside force—God, or the super-conscious mind, or infinite intelligence—as the source of their creativity. New ideas, solutions, the right lines or melodies will just come to you if you allow them to, if you don't think too hard about it. Have you ever been driving along and had a great idea just pop into your head? Or have you been almost asleep or just waking up when some solution comes to you? That's how it works.

The key is to create an environment or frame of mind conducive and open to inspiration, trust that something will happen, get your self out of the way, and then just start. Aaron Copland, the great 20th century composer, said it well: "Inspiration may be a form of the super-conscious or of the subconscious, I wouldn't know. But I am positive that it is the antithesis of self-consciousness." Forget yourself and get into "the flow."

The Truth About Humor (or Vice Versa)

Try as I have in one way or another for nearly 20 years to write comedy, I find that no one has a sense of humor like God. Have you ever seen a platypus? Who but God would put a beak on a beaver? We need only observe.

By that I also mean that truth is always funnier than fiction. And on that note here are a few hilarious, absolutely true stories that have happened in my career and travels that, in my wildest dreams, I could not have imagined.

- One afternoon after a lunchtime program at Monroe County Community College near Detroit, a young guitarist was asking me some questions about playing. After a while he got a serious look and asked, "So, when did you give up on the idea of being famous?" I nodded my head a few times, thought about it for a moment and replied, "Just now."

- During my first year of college one hot Sunday afternoon, I was at the lake with a few friends trying to impress this girl I'd been hanging out with by playing guitar for her. I mean, chicks dig guitar players, right? I played a few parts of some hit songs and she asked, kind-of snobby, "Well, do you play anything all the way through?" Hmmm . . . OK . . . Put off a little, but still trying I played a song all the way through. She then said, "Do you do anything well?" I shot back, "Yeah, everything but choose my dates." Did I mention that I spent a lot of time alone in college?

- When I was a staff songwriter for Sony Music Publishing, on more than one occasion after a show some well-meaning audience member would ask, "Wow, is that a real song or did you write that?" Someday, perhaps I'll write a real song.

- Finally, while at home enjoying some time off the road, I got a call from yet another telemarketer. I was NOT in the mood so I cut her off. "Ma'am, I'm not interested. Thank you. Good bye." As I was hanging up, I could faintly hear her say, "Could I ask you a personal question?" I thought, "Well, this is different." Intrigued with her angle, I played along, "Okay, sure, ask me a personal question." "Do you do concerts at colleges?" she inquired. For 15 years before becoming a corporate entertainer and professional speaker, I played more than 1800 college and university shows. "Well, yes," I replied hesitantly, a bit surprised. Delighted she said, "I knew that was you when your name came up on my computer! I saw you play at Highland Community College in Highland, Kansas a few years ago." I remembered the show! I hadn't met her but I recalled the setting and the audience, and we talked a little about the school and my program. It felt nice to be remembered. She went on to say she had wanted to buy one of my CDs that night but didn't have the money. I said, "Well, if you still want one, I can send you an order form." She said, "Great," gave me her address, and ended up ordering a CD.

I hung up the phone... and then the reality of what had just happened hit me: I just sold something to a telemarketer! Yeah, baby, YEAH! Now I'm empowered. Go ahead, all you telemarketers, call me at home. Try to sell me a new credit card or get me to change my phone service. You will own a Mike Rayburn CD!

About the Author

Mike Rayburn

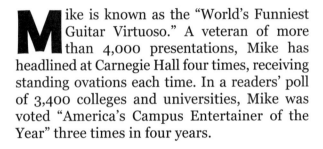

Mike is known as the "World's Funniest Guitar Virtuoso." A veteran of more than 4,000 presentations, Mike has headlined at Carnegie Hall four times, receiving standing ovations each time. In a readers' poll of 3,400 colleges and universities, Mike was voted "America's Campus Entertainer of the Year" three times in four years.

Using his hilarious songs and parodies, his amazing guitar creations, and a contagious zest for life, Mike challenges his audiences to leap beyond their perceived limitations. He draws from experiences as a comedian, adventurer, business owner, author, and philanthropist to deliver presentations that are inspirational and musically amazing.

Contact Information:

Mike Rayburn
Quantum Talent

Phone: 843-839-1668
www.mikerayburn.com

What's So Funny About Stress?

By Andy Hickman, CSP

A letter arrived from the Credit Bureau saying, "Mr. Hickman, we regret to inform you that your application for credit has been denied, because according to our records, you are deceased." Why am I always the last one to know these things?

The letter went on to say, "If you believe that our records are in error, you have 60 days to dispute this matter." I said to myself, "Dispute this matter?! They've gotta be kidding!" So with letter in hand, I went to the office of the Credit Bureau to "dispute this matter." The lobby was filled with other people waiting to dispute their matters, and I wondered how many of them were dead, too. The beige walls and incessant elevator music made me wonder if perhaps I wasn't having a bad Twilight Zone experience. I half expected the counselor that would hear my dispute to be Rod Serling himself.

After an hour, a lady appeared and stated that it was my turn. This lady had the same cheerful expression as all of those other highly motivated civil servants that work at the Department of Motor Vehicles. She asked, "Mr. Hickman, what seems to be the problem?" Handing her my letter, I told her, "Well, what seems to be the problem is that I'm *dead*. You see, according to your records, I am." She asked me to have a seat while she pulled my file. I told her, "I can't sit because after all, I'm dead! I'll just levitate up in the corner of the ceiling." She responded curtly, "This is no laughing matter and you need to be serious." I told her, "I'm dead serious! What could be more serious than being dead and not knowing it?"

I'm pleased to report I got out of that one alive.

Energy Suckers

Speaking of stress, do you have stress? No? Well, maybe *you* don't have stress, but perhaps you know a carrier! You know the kind of person I mean. It's that coworker who always sucks the energy right out of you. Appropriately, I call these sad folks "Energy Suckers."

Energy Suckers seem to have something critical and negative to say about almost any subject. Here's how it goes: You're having a terrific, high-attitude day. You feel jazzed about life; your energy level is smokin'! Then, you see the Energy Sucker coming down the hall. He meets you at the water cooler and says something like, "What are you so happy about? This is a lousy place to work. My boss is an idiot, and my coworkers are morons. I wish the management around here would make up their minds; first they tell me to do it this way and then they change it and make me do it another way. You talk about overworked and underpaid? You're lookin' at it right here!" These pathetic folks carry around a "victim mentality" and feel entitled to complain.

So you enter the encounter feeling super. Then the Energy Sucker plugged into you and sucked out all of your energy. You walk away feeling violated! How did he do that? With the tongue . . . the English language. Look out, because an Energy Sucker can destroy the mood and morale of an entire workplace. By all means, avoid Energy Suckers. And if you can't avoid them, try using these techniques to influence them.

To build workplace morale, use language that encourages others and gives them energy. You can do this by controlling the words that you speak. Depending on the person and the situation, you can deflect the critical attitude of Energy Suckers by giving them a compliment. Say something like, "You're looking fit. Have you been working out?" or "I like what you're wearing. Where do you shop?"

You can be even more direct (and sarcastic) and say, "Here, let me give you a quarter so you can call someone who cares."

Let all Energy Suckers know that you're not going to attend their pity parties. They will soon leave you alone and find someone else to victimize.

To avoid being an Energy Sucker yourself, choose language that adds energy to others. In the process, your own energy increases and the morale of your coworkers improves. To encourage others while on the job, tell them positive things: "I admire your work. It's a privilege working with you. You make work fun. If you need help with that project, I'd be happy to lend a hand." You don't have to gush all over people. Just let them know you notice and appreciate them. An inch of kindness and recognition goes a long way to building a strong, productive work environment.

Buying Animal Crackers

To overcome stress, deal with it like you did when you were a little kid. Remember going to the grocery store with your mom? You probably found the boxes of Animal Crackers and asked her, "May I have those?" Occasionally she'd said, "Sure you can have them" and put a box right into your hands

Now, did you just grab the box and clutch it tightly? Of course not. You held the box by its little string. And as you walked through the store, *you* became the envy of all the other little boys and girls. Holding the box by the string and swinging it communicated in little-kid-speak, "Nah, nah, nah, nah, nah! I've been a good boy!"

Even today, although you're all grown up, there's still something about a box of Animal Crackers that makes you feel good—the colors, the animals, the shape, but most of all the string on the box. I suggest the next time you're having a bad day, go buy yourself some Animal Crackers, then walk back into your office holding the box by the string. Your coworkers will probably sense that you're stressed, but hey, that's okay. You're dealing with it! Just set the box on your desk as a reminder. Even if you never eat them, you'll feel better. Oh, and if you're married, make it a rule that when you fight with your spouse, you both have to be holding your Animal Crackers box by the string. I dare you to continue fighting! Ah, behold the power of the string!

Playing Ball

Here's another stress buster—T-ball. You know the game T-ball, don't you? A baseball is placed on top of a short tee, then little kids wearing little helmets swing over the ball and under the ball. Sometimes they actually hit the ball. When they do, other little kids run around like keystone cops trying to stop the ball and throw it.

Suppose you've had a hard day at work and you're feeling stressed. Then, while driving home, you happen to see a T-ball game being played. Just stop your car and watch. You don't even have to know the kids or their parents to have fun. Get involved. It'll be a hoot.

When my son, Landon, played baseball, he taught me that winning isn't everything, but getting a snow cone after the game just might be!

Yes, I was your typically supportive yet anxious parent. Although I didn't require him to be the best player on the team, I did want him to do his best. So nearly every day, his mom, his sisters, or I would practice with him. Though not the most gifted ballplayer at six years of age, he was easily one of the cutest!

I'll never forget the day he made a big hit and ran around all the bases. Upon reaching home plate, the parent-filled crowd cheered wildly for him saying, "Way-to-go, Landon!" "You're The Man!" and "That's *my* boy!" (Guess who said that!) All the while, Landon just stood there with his feet firmly planted on home plate — basking in the glory of the cheers. Eventually he walked to the dugout to receive more praise from his teammates. But by the last inning, his team was down by three runs and it looked like a loss was inevitable.

Being the competitive person that I am, I found a moment to tell Landon he had to hit another home run in order for his team to win. Using a firm tone of voice, I said, "Now, son, hit the ball down the third-base line to the third baseman. I've been watching this kid and there's no way he's gonna be able to throw you out. Get your bat back. Nice level swing. Look at the ball. Adjust your stance. Bring your leg around. No, not that way, the other way! Son, I said bring your leg around this way!" This is when he spoke the wise words that put it all in perspective: "Chill out, Dad. We're still gonna get the snow cone."

I guess he was right. Often we parents put far too much importance on winning and far too little importance on why our kids are playing in the first place . . . for fun. Landon had his own reasons for playing, not mine. I've learned to respect his point of view and, in the process, I've also learned that rainbow snow cones really are the best.

Three Humor Rules

No one likes following "rules," but here are three I've learned to respect when using humor:

Rule #1: When choosing humor, make certain that *you* are the brunt of the joke, not someone else. During his presidency, Ronald Reagan was a master at using self-deprecating humor to endear himself to the press. Who can forget what he said to his wife Nancy after he had been shot? "Honey, I forgot to duck!"

As a humorist, I get far greater mileage with my audiences when I poke fun at *me* rather than *them*. For example, I was presenting a keynote speech in beautiful Jackson Hole, Wyoming, before a group of 200 Neonatal Nurses. About an hour before I started, I did something that all Certified Speaking Professionals know not to do—I drank *way* too much water.

Thirty minutes into my speech, I started to feel the "urge". . . at the end of my hour I really had to "go!" So, I walked out of the room . . . into the hall . . . and ran to the nearest bathroom. I proceeded to relieve myself, sighing heavily, and then flushed. After doing this, I returned to the meeting room only to discover that all 200 nurses were pointing at me and laughing. I looked down thinking maybe my fly was open but it wasn't. Suddenly I realized why they were laughing—I had forgotten to turn off my wireless microphone! They heard everything! The zip . . . the tinkle-tinkle . . . the sigh . . . and of course the flush. I was so embarrassed! So, I went up to the front of the room, thrust my fists into the air, and shouted, "I feel like a New Man! But I really could use a catheter if you have one." Those nurses understood my humor completely.

Rule #2: Practical jokes can leave behind a bad taste. How did I come to learn this? Keep in mind that I was only eight years old at the time that the following took place:

One evening, my older brother Wendy, a friend named John Klinger, and I were preparing for bed. During our preparations, Wendy applied some stuff to his fingernails that looked like fingernail polish. Actually, it was a *hot* substance used to discourage him from biting his fingernails during the night. In her doggy bed in our room, my mother's Pekingese dog, Sophie, was sleeping soundly, her little tongue barely hanging out of her mouth. I don't remember which one of us three first came up with the idea (surely not me!), but we decided to paint the dog's little tongue with this nasty fingernail stuff. As my brother brushed the hot liquid on Sophie's tongue, the little dog instinctively brought her tongue into her mouth. She quickly developed a pained expression as she tried in vain to rid her mouth of the foul substance. The three of us watched and laughed ourselves silly. John and I egged Wendy on, saying, "Do it again! Do it again!" and Wendy complied. This was so much fun that we rushed to tell my mother all about it.

When she heard the tale, my mother asked, "So, you boys thought that was funny, did you?" Knowing my mother's zeal for justice, I started to get a little worried for the first time.

So the three of us went to bed and fell asleep. Later that night, I was sharply awakened by a burning sensation on my lips. They felt like they were on fire! I licked my lips to quench the fire, but it only made things worse. Now my tongue felt like it was on fire, too. My brother and John were both experiencing the same pain.

All three of us ran into the bathroom looking for water. That's when we saw my mother standing at the doorway with a satisfied look on her face, holding that bottle of fingernail stuff. She had painted it on our lips while we were sleeping! We each got our drinks of water as my mother said, "Oh, that was just so funny!" Needless to say, we learned an important lesson that night. I'm just glad we didn't use Super-Glue!

Rule #3: Resist using (or even listening to) sarcasm, racism, sexism, cynicism, and every other temptation to tear others down. These are sorry substitutes for real humor. Sarcasm, racism, sexism, and cynicism all have a darkness to them that's subversive in nature because they attack the character of others, and are only used by imbeciles who aren't clever enough to find and say something truly funny. They rely on "shock value" because their feeble minds haven't matured beyond the playground or locker room.

The rule of thumb is this: If there's any doubt about the appropriateness of the humor you might use, don't use it! Ask yourself if what you're about to say will compromise your reputation and your influence with those in attendance. A reputation is like a shadow—sometimes it follows you, sometimes it precedes you—but good or bad, it's always with you!

Is your reputation worth risking for a cheap laugh? For what price would you barter your integrity? Chances are good that your conscience is a better guide than an unbridled tongue.

So, to avoid stress, remember to follow the Humor Rules.

Humor Rules

1. Buy some Animal Crackers.

2. Avoid Energy Suckers.

3. Play more T-ball.

4. Most importantly, if you're dead, don't tell the Credit Bureau.

About the Author

Andy Hickman, CSP

Andy is a favorite speaker for most of the Fortune 100 companies in America. Perhaps his most important presentation was to the survivors of the Oklahoma City bombing.

Andy draws on his experience as a businessman who has owned three businesses simultaneously: a mortgage/finance company, a property management group, and a real estate development and construction company.

He honed his skills as a professional illusionist working with David Copperfield's "Project Magic." His keynotes and presentations combine clean humor, amazing magic, and customized messages that move people to action.

He is also the author of *Stuff That Really Matters — Establishing Priorities for Your Business and Your Life.*

Contact Information:

Andy Hickman, CSP
1156 Fairway Dr. West
Lindale, TX 75771

Phone: 800-947-0486
www.andyhickman.com

Icky Happens

by Karyn Buxman, MSN, CSP, CPAE

The bumper sticker read "Sh** happens!" My first thought was, "How rude!" My next thought was, "Thank goodness." From a humorist's point of view, if it wasn't for the pain and stress in the world, what would we laugh about?

> *"There is a thin line that separates laughter and pain, comedy and tragedy, humor and hurt. And how do you know laughter if there is no pain to compare it with?" — Erma Bombeck*

It's my philosophy that most humor comes from pain and discomfort. Maybe it's your own. Maybe it's somebody else's. It might be something major. It could be something minor.

But face it—we're not laughing about having good hair days, sexy figures, or big fat paychecks. We're laughing about the things that make us twitch: The person ahead of us in the express checkout lane with 27 items; the teenager who cleans his room by shoving everything under the bed; the driver who leaves his left turn signal on for 17 miles. Good news! You already have more material for humor than you can probably use in a lifetime!

According to psychologist Steven Sultanoff, there are three primary factors in perceiving a painful event as humorous: Temporal distance (how long ago did it happen?); proximal distance (how far away did it happen and is safety an issue?); and emotional distance (what is your emotional attachment?). I believe the trick in discovering "what's funny about this?" in an unpleasant incident is in manipulating the temporal, physical, and/or emotional distance whenever possible. Here's an example:

Participants were returning from a break and getting settled into their chairs before I continued with the rest of my program. The program planner had expected around 350 people. The good news/bad news was that almost 500 people showed up. Rather than turn people away, the hotel had managed to squeeze more tables and chairs into the room, classroom style, but we were packed like sardines. As usual, the lines in the ladies' restrooms were quite a bit longer than the men's, so as I got started, a few stragglers continued to make their way in.

About five minutes into the program, a well-rounded woman came in and tried to slip into her chair unobtrusively. Unfortunately, she was second row from the front, dead center. She started to squeeze her way through the close-knit rows, knocking into audience members, both in front of and behind her. Trying to wedge her way through the narrow passage, she loudly whispered to those in front of her, "Excuse me," and turned half way around to those behind her, slid further down the row, and burbled, "Pardon me."

This went on for about three excruciating minutes until finally she reached her destination, swept her hands behind her to smooth out her skirt before she plopped into her seat, and then realized that while she was in the ladies' room, she had tucked her skirt into the back of her panty hose!

After the program was over, I was pleasantly surprised to see her amongst the people waiting to talk to me. When she stepped forward, she smiled broadly and said, "Someday I'm gonna laugh about this, right?"

HA! (Humor Activity)

Comedienne and speaker Christine Cashen shares a technique that she calls Pet Peeve Poetry: She takes her pet peeves and petty annoyances and turns them into funny poems. I took her suggestion one step further and put my pet peeves to memorable tunes or Pet Peeve Parodies. Here's an example of one of my pet peeves put to the tune of Twinkle, Twinkle, Little Star:

> Blinker, blinker, little car
> Do you know just where you are?
> With your blinker blinking right,
> And no turnoff that's in sight...
> Blinker, blinker, can't you see?
> That you're driving me crazy!

Go ahead. Give Pet Peeve Poetry or Pet Peeve Parodies a try.

Someday We're Going to Laugh About This

Have you ever said to yourself or to others, "Someday we're gonna laugh about this?" How about shortening the time frame? Granted, some time has to elapse because at the peak of a crisis people aren't ready to laugh. The time that it takes to detach and see the humor varies from person to person and event to event. Did you ever have a moment that was so embarrassing and humiliating that you didn't think you would ever live it down, and then a few days or weeks later you were sharing it with a colleague and laughing about it?

"Someday we'll laugh about this." — Nixon to White House aide

Let's say a guy gets up in front of his sales team to make an important presentation only to find that his zipper is in the down position. He might see the humor in it immediately, crack a comment, and then move on. Or he might feel so embarrassed that he takes out his humiliation on the sales team for weeks to come. How quickly he can emotionally detach from the snafu determines his response.

> **HA!**
>
> Rude drivers make me crazy but there seems to be no shortage of them, especially during rush hour. When someone lays on his horn or gestures offensively, I try to emotionally detach by asking myself if it will make a difference in ten years? Ten months? Ten weeks? Ten days? Ten minutes? Ten seconds? Once things are in their proper perspective, I visualize the driver in his underwear (usually not a pretty sight) and let it go. Try this mental manipulation with your next frustration.

Jane, a client from Arkansas, recently told me that she and her husband were traveling the southwest. During their vacation, she ate something that violently disagreed with her gastrointestinal system with disastrous results. Every time they passed a gas station, Jane's husband would pull the car in and she would rush to the rest room. After numerous stops all morning and afternoon, she was becoming exhausted. Once again her husband whipped into a service station, Jane grabbed the rest room key from the attendant and rushed to the bathroom. Several minutes later she trudged over to the attendant and handed the handsome young man the key to the bathroom. He looked out toward her husband beside their car and asked, "Got gas?"

Without looking up she answered, "No—but this diarrhea is exhausting!"

In the silence that followed, it gradually dawned on Jane, to her utter embarrassment, that he meant had she purchased any gas! Her face turned crimson—and then she burst out laughing. Fortunately the time necessary for her to see the humor in the situation was hardly more than a split second.

Might as Well Laugh . . .

During a spring flood in DesMoines, Iowa, a movie theatre, temporarily underwater, posted the following on their marquee: "No Lifeguard on Duty."

Joke circulating after a series of natural disasters in Los Angeles: What are the four seasons in L.A.? Earthquake, fire, flood, and mudslides.

With gas costs soaring, a station in Madison, Wisconsin posted the following gasoline prices: Unleaded: $1.89; Super Unleaded: Arm; Premium: Leg.

Monologue Material

If it weren't for the icky stuff, what would Leno and Letterman do for their monologues? Granted there'd still be Stupid Pet Tricks and Jay Walking, but the bulk of their comedy stems from the political imperfections, the celebrity slip-ups, and current events calamities. For example, Leno shared the following in one of his monologues:

Rep. Gary Condit hasn't been very forthcoming with the FBI about his involvement with his missing intern. Now it's been revealed that when Clinton was in trouble in '98, he (Condit) wrote a letter to Newt Gingrich demanding that Bill Clinton come forward with full disclosure of what he had done. Only in Washington would a man alleged to have had an affair with an intern, condemn a man who had an affair with an intern, by writing a letter to a man who had an affair with a staffer. God Bless Washington.

"Nothing icky lasts forever." — Deborah Norville

Icky happens. No way around it. It happens on a personal level with obstinate teens or unbalanced check books. It happens at a professional level in the way of cranky coworkers or arrogant bosses. On a community level, it could be wacky weather or political scandals. On a national level, it includes the government, taxes and the stock market. On a worldwide level, we see war, terrorism, and global warming.

In the Dark

Much of the humor we've seen since 9/11 is what's referred to as gallows humor, also known as dark humor, sick humor, or black humor. In her book *Humor and the Health Professions*, nurse researcher Vera Robinson explains that black humor is a coping mechanism we use when we feel out of control and powerless. It is a defense against the dreadfulness about which we are laughing.

> *"When tragedy and death cloud our lives, they darken our humor as well." — Karyn Buxman*

An example of gallows humor came across my desk the other day in the form of an office memo:

ATTN: ALL EMPLOYEES ALERT no: 3011

Recently we have received credible intelligence that there have been seven terrorists working in your office. Six of the seven have been apprehended. Bin Sleepin, Bin Loafin, Bin Goofin, Bin Lunchin, Bin Drinkin, and Bin Ass-Kissin have all been taken into custody.

At this time, no one fitting the description of the seventh cell member, Bin Workin, has been found at your office. We are confident that anyone who looks like he's Bin Workin will be very easy to spot. You are obviously not a suspect at this time. So keep on doing what you Bin Doin.

The challenge: What is stress relieving for some is stress

producing for others. While some find gallows humor to be a positive means of dealing with their stress, others find these expressions of humor to be salt rubbed into an already irritated wound. What's appropriate? What's not? There's no clear-cut answer. Gallows humor can be a positive means of coping with anxiety, but it helps if certain guidelines are followed. I suggest the following to make your humor less risky and keep it a safe B.E.T.:

- ***Establish a Bond*:** Gallows humor is less offensive when there's a bond between the initiator and recipient of the humor. Often this type of "inside humor" is used within certain boundaries of a certain group of people. There's an almost unspoken agreement: "I'll not be offended by your sick humor if you agree not to be offended by mine."

- ***Be aware of the Environment*:** The trick is to keep the humor within the confines of said group. Once the dark humor escapes the confines of the group, it then may become hurtful. Anyone who hears, sees, or experiences the humor is part of the audience, whether you intended them to be or not. Think twice before hitting the "forward" key on an e-mail or blurting out a joke you just heard. Will it be hurtful if unintended audience members intercept?

- ***Be sensitive to the Timing*:** H. G. Wells once said, "The crisis of today is the joke of tomorrow." Generally it takes time for people to see any humor derived from pain or discomfort. Some people never will. Every person's situation is unique and determined by their own set of circumstances and life experiences. Despite its multiple benefits, humor is always risky business. Try as you may to be politically correct, there will almost always be someone waiting in the wings to be offended. The humor or laughter provides an excuse to ventilate about an unspoken and deeper issue. That being said, if you choose to use humor to cope with difficult times and are mindful of the feelings of others, then, more than likely, most folks won't mind if you laugh.

It's All in the Way You See It

"Nothing is either good or bad. 'Tis thinking that makes it so."
— William Shakespeare

During a violent winter storm, I flew into Pittsburgh and hailed a cab. Making small talk, I said to the cabbie, "This weather's a bummer, huh?"

He turned and smiled broadly. "Oh, no way. When the weather is like this, people don't want to get out and drive. They call me. Business is always best in bad weather. I love it!"

I can't say that his perspective made me feel a whole lot better, but it reminded me once again that we can't control many of the circumstances that occur in our day-to-day lives. We can, however, control our responses to those circumstances. Humor is one of the greatest resources we have at our disposal. Don't get me wrong. I'm not saying that humor is the "be all, end all." Every time something catastrophic happens, I wouldn't expect you to double over in a belly laugh. But if you can learn to twist and turn and play with your pain, then you'll see it from a different perspective. And that, my friend, can make all the difference in the world between having a good day and a lousy day.

Exercise: How Could This Be Worse?

This is an exercise in learning to play with your pain. It can be done by yourself or in a small group. (Misery loves company!) Take an unpleasant circumstance. (Start with a minor annoyance. You can work your way up to major disasters with some practice.) Reflect to see if there are any obvious absurdities. If so, start there. If not, pick one aspect of the situation. Now exaggerate it. Probably not that funny yet. Exaggerate it a little further. Don't be afraid to be wacky. No one is grading you on this assignment. You're getting closer. Exaggerate it again—really go for it. Sometimes you'll hit your funny bone right off the bat. Other times it takes more effort. Here's an example:

I was flying to California with a change of planes in Denver. Bad weather was settling in as we waited in a holding pattern for our turn to land. At last we landed and finally deplaned. It was then I discovered my outbound connection was the only plane to take off on time. I ran to the service desk hoping I could quickly get out on another flight. "Take a seat," the agent said without looking up. "It's gonna be about an hour."

I took my seat and then heard her announce on the intercom that it would be at least another hour. Soon after, I heard it delayed yet another hour. And then another, and another, and another, and another. This went on for more than ten hours!

My first reaction was to feel sorry for myself. Sometimes the pity pot feels pretty comfortable. After a while, however, the people who were stranded with me began to make small talk. A question that kept popping up was, "And what do you do for a living?" It seemed totally inappropriate to respond, "I'm a humorist, damn it! Now just leave me alone!"

I removed myself from the group and, meandering through the airport, I asked myself, "How could this be worse?" I realized for the first time how unique this exercise is. What's worse for me might not be worse for someone else. But at that particular moment, I knew that it would be worse for me to be stuck in the Denver Airport and be pregnant. How could it be worse than that?

I could be nine months pregnant. Okay, mildly amusing but how could it be worse?

I could be in active labor. Now I'm getting a picture. So go for it.

I could be stuck in the Denver Airport, nine months

pregnant, in active labor... and my water could be leaking in front of all these strangers!

Whew! That would definitely be worse. I shook my head, smiling, and rejoined the stranded travelers.

For some, the ability to find humor in adversity comes easily. For others, it's a little tougher. If you find yourself in the latter group, don't get discouraged. It will get easier with practice.

Humor is part of a skill set. Granted some folks are naturally gifted. But just because you weren't born a natural pianist wouldn't be reason for you never to try playing the piano. You probably will never perform standup comedy (there's enough competition out there already, for crying out loud!), but you can still hone your humor skills and glean the numerous physical, psychological, and social benefits.

Practice your humor until it becomes a habit, and may the farce be with you!

HA!

now it's your turn. Take a situation that was unpleasant. now mirthfully exaggerate it. now mirthfully exaggerate it again. And again. And again, as needed, until you can put the event in its proper perspective. _____

_____

_____

About the Author

**Karyn Buxman,
MSN, CSP, CPAE**

While in graduate school, Karyn combined her research with the one thing that enabled her to get through an entire day without losing her sanity: humor. Now an international expert on humor, Karyn puts her studies to work through her energy-charged keynotes that entertain, motivate, and educate audiences.

Karyn's "Humor as Life Strategy" techniques have been publicized in national media through magazine articles, talk shows, and radio programs. Her clients include NASA, Mayo Clinic, Ernst & Young, National Association of Insurance Women, Abbott Labs, Lucent Technologies, and many more.

Contact Information:

Karyn Buxman, MSN, CSP, CPAE
HUMORx
P.O. Box 1273
Hannibal, MO 63401-1273

Phone: 573-221-9086
www.humorx.com • E-mail: info@humorx.com

Finding Fault or Finding Fun?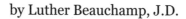

by Luther Beauchamp, J.D.

"**I**'m thirsty!" my three-year-old grandson Joshua kept telling his dad as they traveled down smoke-filled I-95 in northeast Florida during a devastating drought.

"There's no place to stop right now. We'll stop soon."

"But I want something to drink right now."

Trying to get the child's mind off his thirst, his dad asked, "Would you like to sing with Daddy?"

Joshua whined, "But Daddy, I can't sing and cry at the same time."

You can't . . . unless you are a country music singer.

We make the choice every day to sing or to cry. We can look for the positive or the negative. Zig Ziglar said, "It's your *attitude* and not your *aptitude* that determines your altitude."

We can find fault or we can find fun. Some people so diligently and persistently try to find fault, you'd think a reward had been offered for its discovery. Here are several examples of finding the fun in everyday happenings.

Find Fun with Your Family

By finding the fun, we can often turn our pain into joy. One example came from a family event that had rendered mixed emotions.

When my son got married, the wedding ceremony in the church was followed by a reception on the banks of the beautiful Suwannee River. My family has a recreational home there with a picnic shelter, so we decorated the shelter and grounds with tiki torches, palm fronds, and other items to create a Hawaiian luau setting.

A crowd of about 300 friends and family members attended. The food, fellowship—everything—was great. However, in addition to 300 people, about three million sand gnats with hearty appetites for human flesh showed up. We tried many different devices and potions to discourage the hungry insects. The only thing that seemed to work was Right Guard deodorant. I guess it worked, because those critters bit me everywhere except under my arms. Next time, I'll put the deodorant all over my body!

My grandson Joshua—the same one who couldn't "sing and cry at the same time"—continues to provide funny examples. When he was seven, Joshua was playing baseball in the yard along with two boys his age, Kyler and Ryan. Jacob, Joshua's three-year-old brother, thought he was as big as the other boys and joined in. But when their mother Laura heard the younger boy screaming, she went out to rescue him. He'd been hit on the cheek with a bat.

After making sure no bones were broken, Laura turned her attention to the older boys. Ryan, the one who had swung the bat, hurriedly left the scene, supposedly afraid of what Laura might do. Laura later learned from Kyler's mother, who'd arrived on the scene during this critical time, that Joshua caused Ryan's quick departure. Upset about the possibility of serious injury to his little brother, Joshua told Ryan, "I'm gonna take you to court!" As Ryan fled, Kyler told Joshua, "You shouldn't have said that. You don't know how bad court is."

Being a lawyer for the past 35 years, I "know how bad court is." Not only do I try to keep my clients out of court, I enjoy my career as a "humorist" much more than my career as a "legalist."

Find Signs of Fun

Another way to find fun is by reading signs...differently.

One speaker told about seeing instructions by a hotel elevator, "In Case of Fire Do Not Use Elevator." His response was, "That's ridiculous. Who would ever try to put out a fire with an elevator?" That seemed silly enough for me to start looking for different meanings in the written words.

When I saw a sign in front of a fast food restaurant in Alabama that read, "The Big Chicken Sandwich Is Back," two thoughts came to mind. First, I wondered where it had been. Then I was concerned about how long it had been gone.

A Wendy's restaurant in Florida displayed a sign with the message: "We Have Raised the Bar." Since I'm only 5'4" with blisters on both feet, I knew it wouldn't be a good place for me because the last time I was in a Wendy's, it was already difficult for me to see over the bar.

In a conference center cafeteria in Florida, I saw a machine that dispensed beverages including iced tea, lemonade, root beer, and cola. One valve was marked "Iced Tea, Sweetened with Lemon." Until that time, I was totally unaware we could sweeten tea with lemon.

While working on my first book *I'll Try to Be Short*, I attended an authorship skills workshop at the headquarters of the National Speakers Association in Tempe, Arizona. My wife and 22-year-old son Lance had come with me to enjoy a mini-vacation. While staying in the hotel, Lance and I went to the exercise room because I like to watch people exercise. The sign on the wall read, "For Emergency Dial 555." We wondered who would ever want an emergency enough to call for one.

Being alert for ways to interpret signs differently can help us enjoy life and make it more fun for other people at the same time.

Find Fun in the News

Newspapers sometimes intentionally use puns in headlines but other times actual errors show up that result in funny or even embarrassing messages.

My local paper carried an advertisement for a two-bedroom home on a large lot selling for $45,000.00. The ad included a statement, "Won't Last Long!" The question came to my mind, "Why would anyone want to pay that much money for something that won't last long?"

I found this in a supermarket flyer. One of the specials was supposed to be "Country Fried Chicken" but instead read "Country Fried Children."

Among my all-time favorite headlines is one I saw in the Florida Baptist Witness, a weekly newspaper. Each year, there's a statewide push to raise money for the Baptist Children's Homes on Mother's Day. The headline read,

"Mother's Day: A Time for Remembering Mom and Hurting Children." After lunch was over that Mother's Day, I told my family, "We've remembered Mom; now it's time to hurt the children."

Find Fun With Your Failings

Our own activities, mistakes, and lack of attention can result in funny consequences. Being willing to tell these "jokes" on ourselves can be a way of sharing some fun and illustrating some powerful messages.

A few years ago, I was seated next to the aisle during the morning worship service in our church. My wife plays a clarinet in the orchestra, which gives her a good excuse not to sit with me during the worship service. Just as the pastor got up to preach, I reached into my coat pocket and got a piece of hard candy, which on that day happened to be a root beer barrel. My attempt to unwrap it became frustrating, as I was probably turning it opposite from its twist. A tap on my shoulder caused me to turn to the aisle and see an usher kneeling there. In a whisper, he said, "They need one of them in the nursery."

Looking at my root beer barrel, I thought, "They do not need a piece of hard candy in the nursery. A small child could choke to death on something like this. Besides, this is my last root beer barrel." So I looked back at the usher and asked, "What?"

"They need one of them in the nursery," repeated the usher in a whisper that was clearly understood.

My Bible was in my lap, but I couldn't imagine they needed that in the nursery. In the pew rack in front of me was a hymnal, but they wouldn't need that either. Turning back to the usher, I asked again, "They need *what* in the nursery?"

The patient but bewildered usher said, "Tom or his wife."

Seated to my immediate left were a young father and mother whose child was screaming his or her lungs out in the nursery while I was sitting there trying to protect my root beer barrel.

That true story illustrates the importance of real communication. I heard the words clearly but because I was distracted, I was unable to receive the message. We need to make sure that we hear and understand what people are saying rather than just having our auditory receivers record the words.

Find Fun About Yourself

"Stand up, Luther! Oh, you are standing up."

I've heard that line many times. Nearly everyone notices that my height is below that of the average American male. But rather than allow that to crush my self-esteem or otherwise handicap my relationship to others, I have turned the apparent liability into an asset.

During a board meeting, which was sometimes a meeting of the "bored," I knew that when it came time for me to give my report, someone would utter the "Stand up, Luther" line. That's when I first used my now-standard opening line, "I'll try to be short." That remark met with laughter, and I followed with, "How am I doing so far?"

When people realize we can laugh at ourselves—particularly about those things that make us different—they seem more able to accept and appreciate us. Receiving a favorable response to my self-deprecating humor fueled my desire for more. I was inspired to create the following "short-liners" relating to my height, or lack thereof:

- "While researching my genealogy, I learned that my family tree is a Bonsai."

- "I could tell you something off the top of my head but you may want it from a higher source."

- "I don't wear cowboy boots because I can't bend my knees when I do."

- "When I wear a cowboy hat, it makes me look like a mushroom."

- "I thought I had a hearing problem, but after a thorough examination, the doctor reported, 'Your problem is that most of the sound waves are going over your head.'"

- "Being short puts me in a position to give early flood warnings."

- "Never sell yourself short. I don't need the competition."

Other short-liners I use to poke fun at myself include:

- "My Grandpa Callaway was a wit and I inherited half of it."

- "I'm no ordinary lawyer. I would have to improve a lot to become ordinary."

- "My wife doesn't like me to sing in the shower. It leaves a ring around the tub."

- "Because I am a lawyer, speaker, and author, you could say that much of my life has been devoted to wordy causes."

- "Technology is not my best area. I still don't understand how wheelbarrows and scissors work."

As long as we can laugh at ourselves, we will never run out of material.

Find Fun–Your Turn

I hope your own stories came to mind as you read about mine. Childhood and adult experiences furnish fertile fields for funny findings.

Martha Bolton, staff writer for Bob Hope for 15 years, advises in her book, *I Think, Therefore I Have a Headache!*: "Read all the humor books you can get your hands on. Watch comedies. Watch cartoons. Watch politicians."

By finding fun instead of fault, you'll be recognized as an upbeat rather than a beat-up person.

About the Author

Luther Beauchamp, J.D.

A short lawyer with a tall sense of humor, Luther delights his audiences every time. Luther's two books, *I'll Try to Be Short...* and *Legal Shorts...Not Briefs*, are collections of humorous stories from Vanderbilt Law School, 30+ years of law practice, and his life experiences.

In addition to his inspirational messages loaded with humor, Luther presents humor-filled seminars on estate planning. Here's what one client said: "His material is side splitting funny as is. But he did his homework. He weaved in bits and pieces about our company and key individuals that made folks feel like he was part of the family."

Contact Information:

Luther Beauchamp, J.D.
Laughter's Chief Counsel
P. O. Box 10
Chiefland, FL 32644

Phone: 888-568-6677
www.LutherBeauchamp.com • Legalaugh@aol.com

Ordinary Magic:
Life is Fun and Funny— and Filled with Magic

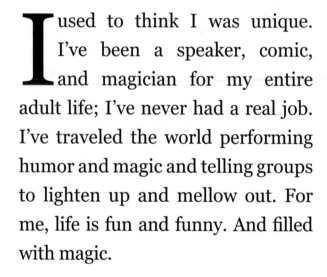

by Brad Montgomery, CSP

I used to think I was unique. I've been a speaker, comic, and magician for my entire adult life; I've never had a real job. I've traveled the world performing humor and magic and telling groups to lighten up and mellow out. For me, life is fun and funny. And filled with magic.

I tend to see humor, joy, hilarity, and magic everywhere. I see it at work and at the grocery store. I notice it while I'm in my car and while I'm at home with my kids. I used to think this magical perspective I had on the world was something I was born with.

But through the years, I've realized that this perspective is available to each and every one of us, and is completely learnable. I've come to understand that what I call "magic" is actually quite ordinary. Anybody can learn Ordinary Magic. And all of us *should*.

What is Ordinary Magic?

To understand Ordinary Magic, it's best to start by telling you what it isn't. Ordinary Magic isn't the tricks magicians do on stage. Because those aren't magic — they're just tricks. (While we're on the subject, the Easter Bunny is a bit iffy, too.)

Here's the real secret this magician loves to share: Magic is a feeling. Ordinary Magic is that feeling you get when you find a five-dollar bill in an old pair of jeans. Or when you taste that first delicious sip of coffee in the morning. Or when you run late for an appointment, yet all the traffic lights magically turn green and the normally over-crowded parking lot has an open space for you—right in front!

Ordinary Magic results from all the little "stuff" throughout the day—and throughout our lives—that puts us in a good mood. It's good luck, a beautiful sight, a wonderful smell, a nice feeling. Ordinary Magic is anything that makes us say, "How cool is that?!"

Who Cares?

You might be thinking, "Yeah, yeah. Magic is a feeling, yada yada, blah blah. What has this got to do with me? Who cares?"

We care about Ordinary Magic because it makes our lives worth living. It makes day-to-day happenings exciting, interesting, and joyful. It adds fun to our lives. And to my way of thinking, fun is what it's all about. Our job in life is not *just* to cross the garden; it's to cross it and *enjoy* the trip. We stop to smell the flowers because it adds to the fun. It makes our lives more magical.

Big Events are Magical. Duh!

We already know the huge events of our lives—promotions, weddings, big vacations, parties, and births—feel magical. But, as exciting and important as these events are, our lives are mostly made up of the day-to-day stuff. The getting-by stuff. The just-plain-existing stuff. Although the calendar is sprinkled with holidays, there are (obviously) many more days that are just . . . well . . . days. We spend much of our time working, driving our kids to soccer practice, taking care of the yard, shopping at the grocery store—the straightforward stuff. But Ordinary Magic can make these routine events exciting, interesting, important—and, of course, fun.

For example, I remember taking my oldest daughter, Claire, to the garden center when she was three. She loves to eat tomatoes so I thought it would be fun to buy some plants for our back yard.

At the store, we started by staring at the tomato plant display. I questioned the advantages of the Beef Steak versus Early Girl varieties. Claire just stared at the plants. I wondered if it was worth buying the big plants for $12—the ones with little tomatoes already on them—or if we should get the cheap six-pack of tiny plants with no fruits yet. Claire kept staring. Then I considered the importance of fertilizer. Claire finally couldn't contain herself any longer. She pulled on my hand and excitedly shouted, "Daddy! Daddy! Daddy! Guess what! Guess what! Tomatoes grow . . . on plants!"

Claire was right. It's very cool—magical even—that tomatoes grow on plants. It's fun that we can buy them, plant them, and watch them grow. As an adult, I took the whole experience for granted. But my daughter reminded me that magic surrounds us, even during errands to the garden store. If we don't spend effort and energy enjoying the day-to-day parts of our lives, we're missing out on the magic available to us *all the time.*

Three Types of People

The old joke says something like, "There are three types of people: Those who are good at math and the other kind." Of course, we all know this is silly and that there must be a *fourth* group: Those who don't care about math because they own calculators.

But with Ordinary Magic, it clearly comes down to two groups. The first group consists of people who cannot see any magic . . . period. We know folks like this—we're usually seated next to one of them at big family feasts. They see doom and gloom everywhere. When asked how they're doing, they actually tell all those who will listen their dreary stories. "My rash is back; my grown kids are a bunch of classless louts; my job is boring; my car smells bad; I hate this hot weather." Yada yada yada. They are down, and they do their best to pull us down with them. After spending time with them, we feel like taking a shower.

The other group consists of people who are upbeat, optimistic, enthusiastic, and excited. Life is great, the weather's wonderful, they love (at least parts of) their jobs, they enjoy what they do and the people they're around. Those in this second group naturally understand the concept of Ordinary Magic.

Here's the really good news: We get to *choose* to which group we want to belong. Amazing! Magic! If we fail to see (or worse, if we ignore) those tiny moments of everyday joy, we find ourselves drained, stressed, and humorless. But the opposite is equally true: By simply looking out for and focusing on wonderful moments, feelings, and events, our lives become more magical.

Putting Ordinary Magic into Life

To fill our lives with the Ordinary Magic, all we have to do is *notice* it. I did something recently that reminded me what happens when we do. I bought a minivan—and learned a lesson, too. (Buying a mini-van isn't easy; in fact, it's *very* hard to spend that much money on a car you don't want.)

Cars have never been one of my hobbies. As long as my car starts, has a comfy seat, sports a great radio and as many buttons as possible, I don't care what's under the hood. (Hey! Just because I'm not a car guy doesn't mean I'm not a buttons kinda guy!)

I'm *especially* not a minivan guy. Until recently, I barely knew they existed; they were practically invisible to me.

But then, when my wife, Kim, and I found ourselves in the market to buy a minivan, all that changed. I noticed minivans on the roads *everywhere*! I went from never even seeing one to not being able to step off the curb without almost being run over by one.

It's a common phenomenon: Things that have been there all along only become visible when we decide to look for them. Ordinary Magic is no different. If you don't see magic now, just open your eyes and deliberately hunt for it. And when you do—put on your seatbelt and get ready for a fun ride.

Ever notice that Kids Always notice?

I have three kids—one of each. A boy, a girl, and the kind with a calculator! (Sometimes, you should even look for magic in stupid jokes.) One of the things I love most about kids—aside from the tax deduction—is that they see the world as a magical place all the time. They don't have to try; they just do it.

Take my son, Ben. Please. Nobody can find Ordinary Magic like this kid. Ben's favorite game is "Chase." He loves this simple game: I chase Ben and he runs away like a crack-crazed idiot on laughing gas, screaming, giggling, and waving his arms. (With my little boy, Chase is a very *loud* game.)

One day we were playing Chase, with Ben doing his customary careening across the lawn, totally absorbed in this game, screaming and shouting and laughing all the way. Then without warning—or any apparent reason—he stopped. And I mean suddenly stopped. It was as though somebody turned off a switch.

He yelled at me, "Daddy! Freeze!" I stopped. (It was either that or run over the little guy.) Ben quietly kneeled down and picked a dandelion that had gone to seed. With a huge, cheek-puffing blow, his breath sent the seeds flying through the air. He stood still in silence as the wind carried them away.

"OK, Daddy. Wheeeeeeeeeeee!" And he was off again! The switch had turned back on. He was playing Chase as though he hadn't ever stopped.

Then it was my turn to be curious. "Ben, stop. Whoa! Let me ask you, why'd you blow away the dandelion seeds? What was that all about?" That's when Ben proved that sometimes three year olds are the wisest of all. He said, "Daddy, I always do that."

Ben understood. He got it. He was smart in the way that only children can be smart. Ben was, and always has been, on the lookout for Ordinary Magic. I'll never forget the lesson Ben taught me that day: *Not only should we stop and smell the flowers, we should also pay close attention to members of the broad-leaf weed family.*

Thinking back, I must have stepped over that stupid dandelion two or three times before Ben picked it out. Given the chance, I would have stepped over it dozens of times without even noticing it. And even if I did see it, I would have recognized it for what it was—a weed. A blemish. Something to be ignored. Something to get rid of. Something to kill.

But because Ben is used to looking for the joy in life (except when he hasn't had his afternoon nap, or when his sister steps on his train, or when you tell him to get cleaned up for dinner, or . . .), he couldn't miss that dandelion. He saw it as a toy. An opportunity for fun. A chance at joy. He saw the dandelion as magic. Certainly he couldn't have ignored it.

Think about it for yourself. What dandelions are you ignoring?

It's So Obvious, It Sounds Stupid

With Ordinary Magic, we not only notice things that put us in a good humor; we pass over the yucky stuff. If we're busy celebrating the fact that the glass is half full, it's hard to whine about it being half empty.

My wife, Kim, reminded me of this point recently when I found my nephew, my son, and one of my daughters in the bathroom. (None of these kids is older than six.) They were painting their fingernails and toenails an assortment of colors, and were really proud of the color "patterns" they'd created. But they had spilled three different bottles of fingernail polish all over the counter, part of the wall, and the floor.

I stormed into the bathroom and got mad. I didn't see any Ordinary Magic in this scene. Highly annoyed, I hollered at the kids, and then I got some towels and started cleaning, using up most of my wife's nail-polish-remover just to clean the baseboards. The kids, meanwhile, ignored me and continued to giggle away, happily trying to finish each other's toes.

Kim came to see what the commotion was about, and started laughing. She didn't just snicker—she went for all-out hysteria. I became even more annoyed. Obviously, she didn't notice how our baseboards were going to reflect "Coral Sunset" forever, how the boys were looking suspiciously *sassy*, how she was going to have to buy a brand new bottle of polish remover—how terrible it all was.

When I grumped at her, she made my own point perfectly by saying, "Brad, why don't you mellow out, lighten up, and follow the advice you tell your audiences every day?"

She was right. The kids looked adorable as they giggled. Not only had they painted their nails, they'd covered half their fingertips, too. The bathroom smelled like a chemical factory, but the fingernail polish remover was working fine (and it's cheap!). This was one of those fun and funny parent moments, and I missed it. I got bogged down in the mess and failed to notice the Magic. But Kim got it. She focused on the laughter, on their goofy nails, and on the whole silly situation.

It's Almost Too Simple

I realize this Ordinary Magic concept seems oversimplified. I know our lives—both at work and at home—are complicated. The front page of the newspaper reminds us we live in a thorny, complex, and dangerous place. Life can be hard, stressful, and filled with potholes. And, yeah, many of our problems are a tad more serious than spilled fingernail polish.

But the amazing and truly magical part is this: Life really is that simple. It isn't *easy*, but it's simple. Even during the most difficult times, we find magic in our choices. In every situation, we can either focus on the misery, or concentrate on the magic. We can wallow in our challenges or we can search for joy.

How do you change your life? The answer is simple: Search for, discover, and enjoy Ordinary Magic.

I'm not Unique

I've been lucky because my job as a professional funny person has helped me to see that life is fun, funny, and filled with magic. I'm lucky in that seeing the amusing side of things has (almost) always been easy for me. And as I said before, I used to think that this outlook made me unique.

But that's not true. Ordinary Magic is accessible to each and every one of us. All of us can—and should—look for, notice, and enjoy a magical life. And I ask you, "How cool is that?!"

About the Author

Brad Montgomery, CSP

Brad never planned to be a business humorist; he planned to be a lawyer. He decided to be a comic and magician for a while, then "get serious." To date—as a hilarious motivational speaker and corporate entertainer—he's still waiting to "get serious."

Brad urges audience members to notice how their lives are filled with humor and magic. His programs are very funny, and leave his audiences with springs in their steps, and good feelings about themselves, the meeting, and the future.

He's cracked-up folks in 47 states and on four continents. And although he's proud of his many awards and national credits, he's convinced his best "tricks" are his wife and three small kids.

Contact Information:

Brad Montgomery, CSP
Brad Montgomery Productions
Denver, CO

Phone: 800-624-4280
E-mail: brad@bradmontgomery.com
www.BradMontgomery.com

humor me

Some More!

Still Craving More?

Lookin' for free articles, jokes, gags and humor ideas? Need to buy some hilarious props, toys and gags to spice up your workplace? Do you need a coach to help you with your presentations? Are you in the market for more books, tapes, CDs or DVDs about humor and laughter?

What can you do? Where can you go?

Put this book down right now and visit ALL of the authors' websites. They are chock-full of resources—and other funny stuff—you can use to add humor to your life. Stuff that will make you smile; things that will make you laugh. (You can even buy more copies of this book!)

Need someone to come to you and make your group laugh?

Does your company have a meeting? An annual event?

Do you attend a convention that could benefit from one of these very funny motivational speakers?

Please contact the authors to learn about how they can help you to add the power of laughter to your convention, meeting, or program.

List of author web sites on next page.

Michael D. Aronin. . . . . www.MichaelAronin.com

Luther Beauchamp, JD . . . . . www.LutherBeauchamp.com

Karyn Buxman, MSN, CSP, CPAE . . . . www.Humorx.com

June Cline, CSP. . . . . www.JuneCline.com

Ronald P. Culberson, MSW, CSP . . . www.FUNsulting.com

Scott Friedman, CSP. . . . . www.FunnyScott.com

Tim Gard, CSP. . . . . www.TimGard.com

Izzy Gesell, MS Ed, CSP . . . . www.IzzyG.com

Andy Hickman, CSP . . . . www.AndyHickman.com

Mark Mayfield, CSP, CPAE . . . . . . www.MarkMayfield.com

Brad Montgomery, CSP . . . . . . www.BradMontgomery.com

Brad Nieder, M.D. . . . . www.HealthyHumorist.com

Kathleen Passanisi, PT, CSP   www.KathleenPassanisi.com

Mike Rayburn . . . . www.MikeRayburn.com

Greg Risberg,MSW, CSP . . . . www.GregRisberg.com

Craig Zablocki . . . . www.PositivelyHumor.com